7 Steps to Financial Freedom

7 Steps to Financial Freedom

SIMPLE HABITS
COMPOUNDED RETURNS

MANEESH TANEJA

Konark Publishers Pvt. Ltd
206, First Floor
Peacock Lane, Shahpur Jat
New Delhi - 110 049
+91-11-4105 5065
india@konarkpublishers.com, us@konarkpublishers.com
www.konarkpublishers.com

The author holds the copyright of all the illustrations.
Illustrations that storyboard the content of each chapter have been done by Mr Shivanshu Kumar. Shivanshu's Instagram handle is @shivanshukrr.

ISBN: 978-81-993018-8-7

Edited by Preeta Priyamvada
Cover design by Syed Dilshad Ali
Typeset by Saanvi Graphics, Noida
Printed and bound in India by Thomson Press India Private Limited

Dedicated to My Parents

Dad, I miss you. Mom, where would I be without you.

Disclaimer

This book and its content are for educational purposes only. They constitute the author's opinions. Data used in this book is from public sources and is for illustrative purposes. The book or any of its parts should not be considered investment advice. Readers are advised to do their own due diligence and seek professional help before they start investing.

Data used for tables and the calculation of portfolio returns has been sourced from the following websites:

www.nsiindia.gov.in
www.nseindia.com
www.goldprice.org
www.icicidirect.com
www.macrotrends.net
www.amfiindia.com
www.bseindia.com

Sakshi's Joy Foundation

All royalties from the sale of this book will go to Sakshi's Joy Foundation.

Sakshi's Joy Foundation helps underprivileged paediatric cancer patients access lifesaving treatment at RGCIRC, New Delhi and Tata Memorial Hospital (TMH), Mumbai.

Set up in October 2023, the foundation has helped 33 underprivileged paediatric cancer patients.[*]

Sakshi, a joyful, loving and kind young girl with an enviable sense of humour, was an aspiring theatre artist.

She was 15 years old when she was diagnosed with a rare and aggressive sarcoma called Desmoplastic Small Round Cell Tumour (DSRCT). During the year and a half of her treatment, she endured multiple minor surgeries, an 8 hours long abdominal surgery, brain surgery, 14 rounds of chemotherapy, brain and abdominal radiation; and in the last 3 months slowly lost 90% of her ability to walk, see and hear. None of this could stop her from cracking jokes, imitating celebrities (she was a fantastic mimic), planning her future, getting crowned as prom queen or adding make-up items to her Sephora shopping cart up until a few hours before the cardiac arrest that resulted in her coma and passing away on 6 July 2022, aged 16.

---

[*] Data as on 28 February 2026.

On 25 October 2023, on what would have been her 18th birthday, Sakshi's Joy Foundation was born.

Sakshi's Joy Foundation is a Section 8 Charitable Company {CIN U86100GA2023NPL016154}. All donations to the foundation are entitled to exemption under section 80G(5)(i) of the Income Tax Act, 1961.

You can find out more about Sakshi's Joy Foundation on www.sakshisjoy.org

I would rather have lucky generals than good ones.[†]
Napoleon Bonaparte

कर्मण्येवाधिकारस्ते मा फलेषु कदाचन ।
मा कर्मफलहेतुर्भूर्मा ते सङ्गोऽस्त्वकर्मणि ॥

Shrimad Bhagavad Gita Chapter 2 Verse 47

You have a right to perform your prescribed duties, but you are not entitled to the fruits of your actions.
Never consider yourself to be the cause of the results of your activities, nor be attached to inaction.[‡]

---

† The quote captures a sentiment often attributed to Napoleon Bonaparte. There is no historical evidence of Napoleon having used the phrase 'Give me lucky generals'.

‡ I have used www.holy-bhagavad-gita.org as my source for the shlok and google translate for the English Translation.

Contents

Advance Praise

'For years, people had stayed away from capital markets after hearing news of significant sums of money being lost on account of uninformed investment decisions. Help is at hand. In this book, Maneesh Taneja lays out, in a reader-friendly fashion, the elements that make for informed investing. Those venturing into the markets for the first time and those who have been around and not gained, will benefit equally from this book.'

—**M. Damodaran**, former Chairman, Securities and Exchange Board of India

'An often-overlooked truth about money is that it is deeply personal. It shapes our aspirations, our anxieties, and even the choices we believe are available to us. Yet, many of us approach investing with hesitation, not because of a lack of ambition, but because the path often feels full of jargon, noise, and conflicting opinions. *7 Steps to Financial Freedom* cuts through that clutter with refreshing clarity. Maneesh draws on his invaluable experience of advising investors to show that good financial decisions are not the result of complexity, but of understanding a few essential principles and applying them consistently.

'The book stands out for its focus on building the right habits rather than chasing the right moments. It brings to life ideas that truly define long-term financial success such as balancing risk, committing to asset allocation, respecting the miracle of compounding, preparing for uncertainty, and recognising when professional advice adds meaningful value. Above all, it reminds us that financial freedom is not a destination achieved through wealth alone, but through control, discipline, and the ability to live well within our means. *7 Steps to Financial Freedom* is for anyone who wants to take charge of their money with confidence and clarity.'

—**Vishal Kapoor**, Chief Executive Officer, Bandhan Mutual Fund

'Most personal finance books are theoretical and preachy. *7 Steps to Financial Freedom* is a rare book that is crisp and concise. It combines the absolute essentials of investing for one's financial wellbeing, the what with the how of actually implementing it.'

—**Aashish P. Somaiyaa**, Chief Executive Officer, WhiteOak Capital Asset Management Company

'Maneesh Taneja's book has all the material that you always wanted to know but were afraid to ask. Maneesh explains lucidly how retail investors can benefit from understanding and employing concepts like financial planning, asset allocation, diversification, understanding risk return trade-offs, etc. in their financial journey to reach the ultimate goal – financial independence.'

—**Samir Arora**, Founder & Group CIO, Helios Capital

'*7 Steps to Financial Freedom* is a commendable and timely effort by a practitioner in the field of financial planning and wealth management to synthesize years of knowledge gathering and practical experience into an easy-to-read book. Such a book is timeless in its relevance, but even more so now in an era where we are seeing a significant broadening of participation by individual investors in the financial markets (both in India and globally). The importance of financial planning cannot be stressed enough at a time when job uncertainty amid AI led disruption is a real thing.

'Maneesh rightly begins the book with a chapter on Risks – probably the single most important factor which investors in general and new investors in particular do not pay as much attention to. Part of the reason is that the concept of Risk is intangible (e.g. how do market swings affect your mental wellbeing) and the risks may/may not materialise. The biggest difference between good investors and the rest is an understanding of when to take risk and when not to. He then takes readers on a journey of asset allocation and diversification across assets. For all investors, this is the single biggest determinant of the success of their investment activities. Maneesh adds in a lot of practical examples to make these concepts clearer and bring quantification and tangibility to the subject. The rest of the book helps prepare the investor to strike a balance between spending, saving and investing – again with a lot of practical inputs on how to achieve this troika in everyday life.

'Maneesh's day job makes him a first-hand observer of the growth of financial markets investing by a new breed of investors across the length and breadth of India. Having also worked with some of the most sophisticated investors in the past – it allows him to bring a wealth of expertise to this field!

'Happy reading AND implementing!'

—**Debashish Bose**, Founder, Infinite Circles

Tables and Figures

Tables

Figures

Acknowledgements

This book wouldn't have been possible without the faith of everyone who has ever entrusted me with the responsibility of managing their money. If you are reading this and have ever given me a chance to review your portfolio, Thank You.

Thank you to Mr Rakesh Chopra and Vikas Bhadoria. Every conversation and meeting I have had with you has made me a better version of who I am. Thank you to Ms Amita Batra and Dr Sudhir Kumar Rawal. Your unstinted support and trust are cherished every day. Thank you to Manish Kothari, my sounding board for ideas and a collaborator over the years. To Ashish Grover, colleague at ZFunds, for helping with the research for this book. Thank you to Jalaj Varshney, also a colleague at ZFunds, for helping with the design of the probability-impact matrix.

Thank you to Harsh Gupta for the Foreword and for stimulating my thoughts with ideas over the years. Thank you to all my colleagues in the wealth management industry; you have been the best teachers I could have hoped for.

The first draft of this book was read by dear friends Arunkumar Rajasekaran, Madhura Chikhalikar and sibling Dr Shilpa Parnami. Thank you to each one of them for their patience, indulgence and feedback. I hope I have done justice to your time and effort.

Thank you to Sai Narayan, marketer avant-garde. Thank you to Mr K.P.R. Nair, Ms Priyanka Misra and my editors at Konark Publishers for guiding a novice.

Thank you to Tessie and Sylvain Crouzat for long hours of conversations, for feeding my mind with ideas and the body with sumptuous meals over the years. My band of brothers Zubair Ahmed Kaleem, Sandeep Bajpai, Sushil Shah, G.V. Sanjeev Kumar and Prashant Iyengar – I am at it and I promise I will always be at it.

Dear friends Pooja Sharma, Shivaani Grover and Gaurav Malhotra – thank you for always being there. The single malts, the meals and the green tea can never be celebrated enough. Thank you to Rahul Singh Arya, Akshat Tamot, Pushpendra Sharma, Venkat Raman and Manasi Kutty – Bharat Bhawan, BSS College, Indian Coffee House, Gokul Sweets, Thakur Ji tea stall; Bhopal rocks I say. To Master Kabir Narayanan and his Appa Siddhartha Narayanan for making it all worth the effort.

Hey Myra, Dad wrote a book:)

Foreword

The great Polish composer Chopin once remarked: 'Simplicity is the highest goal, achievable when you have overcome all difficulties. After one has played a vast quantity of notes and more notes, it is simplicity that emerges as the crowning reward of art.'

Maneesh's book also contains many notes of sublime simplicity. He has been able to pen his work accordingly, drawing on his vast experience in helping clients of all types deal with all things wealth. After having played a vast number of notes, he now brings one crowning reward in the form of this book. The reward being as much for the reader as for the writer.

Financial literacy, after all, is of utmost importance for all men and women; and yet it is the one subject that is not properly, if at all, taught in our schools and colleges. We teach our kids trigonometry and Deccan history, which is all very well, but we do not tell them how to think about money. Or even more so, their emotions – be it about finances, or otherwise.

That is a great pity. While many initiatives are now underway, Maneesh's book comes as a great aid in that larger movement. What stands out is his utter practicality and a complete lack of kitsch. So much so that Maneesh has even named this book as *7 Steps to Financial Freedom*, a name so formulaic that only someone with deep subject matter expertise would not feel the need to embellish it with a catchier title.

We must remember that India's median age is less than thirty; it is the fastest growing major economy of the world; it already has one of the best performing stock markets in the world over the last generation, whereas China with even higher economic growth has underperformed in its capital markets as it has had a more bank/property heavy model.

It follows, then, that for many Indians today what they do with their personal finances could be make-or-break for their life goals. In countries where growth is low and people already older, your investment decisions could change your trajectory only so much. In India, the divergence can be enormous.

As millions of Indians begin their investment journey for the first time, the difference between good and bad outcomes will lie not in stock tips or clever products, but in the understanding of first principles. Compounding is not merely a mathematical idea; it is a behavioural one. It rewards steadiness. It punishes haste. It transforms modest, consistent acts into life-changing results.

Maneesh's central message is simple: in a fast-growing country, being what I call 'long India' is both rational and rewarding, but it must be done with structure. Growth alone does not guarantee financial security; discipline does.

Our markets will rise over decades, but they will do so in unpredictable bursts, punctuated by falls and shocks. Those who stay invested, diversify sensibly and match their assets to their goals will benefit the most from India's long arc of economic expansion.

Across the book, Maneesh distils years of managing money for families across incomes and professions. He takes an approach rooted not in jargon, but in clarity: understand risk, diversify across assets, respect time horizons, rebalance periodically, protect yourself from low-probability shocks and stay invested long enough for compounding to work.

These ideas may sound basic, yet they are routinely ignored. The cost of ignoring them can be a lost decade or worse; the benefit of following them can be a secure lifetime for you and your loved ones.

Indeed, a very important point the book makes is about behaviour. India's rising prosperity brings with it an explosion of choice: EMIs, instant credit and the temptation to spend tomorrow's income today. The antidote is not austerity but awareness: knowing that the path to financial freedom depends more on controlling expenses than on chasing higher incomes.

Another theme that resonates is the need for sound advice. In a world overflowing with content, noise often masquerades as knowledge. A good financial adviser provides something algorithms cannot: judgement, context and accountability. End-users of said advice should always understand how the incentives of any advisor are aligned.

The book is an excellent guide for anyone seeking clarity amid noise, and structure amid volatility. It offers a framework that is simple, robust and transformative.

As India and the broader world compounds, so can you and so you should. These seven steps show you how to do it.

Harsh Gupta Madhusudan, CFA, Investor and Author

Introduction

Hello Dear Reader,

Here I am and here is another book on personal finance. If you are reading this, you are someone who is interested in investing, making a suitable return on your money and not just saving it. You are someone who worries about their financial health as much as their physical health and finds the world of finance as complicated as the world of medicine. You try and do your best. Follow the conventional wisdom. You try to avoid sugar and fried food, exercise as often as you can and keep an eye on your weight. You have a life insurance policy, fixed deposits in the bank, some mutual fund investments and there is a good chance that in the last five years you have opened a de-mat and a trading account.

So why the worry? You worry because health, physical and financial, is critical to your existence and has enough variables for you to feel lost and seek assistance and assurance.

I have been a wealth manager for over 17 years. In this period, I have reviewed finances and portfolios of over 1000 families. There are lessons I have learnt as I have helped people achieve their financial goals. I will share these lessons with you in this book. The concepts I will discuss are easy to understand and I suppose you already have an intuitive understanding of these concepts. You practice them in your day-to-day life. This book will help you achieve your financial goals without you having to get an advanced degree in finance or a certificate of graduation from an Ivy League

business school. The framework discussed is easy to implement, all it needs is your time and attention.

But why a book? All that you need to know about personal finance can be learnt from 'FinInfluencers'. There is nothing that you will read in this book that cannot be found on YouTube or on an Instagram Reel. You only have to look, albeit look hard. The reason I say you will have to look hard is because we live in the age of the Creator Economy. Technology has made broadcasters out of us. It has never been easier to post a picture or put a reel on Instagram, start a YouTube channel and release videos or record a conversation on your phone and publish it as a podcast. Access to broadcast tools differentiates us from those who never lived in the twenty-first century. We have tools to tell the world what we think, any time of the day; the whole world is our stage. But with great power comes great competition. How does one stand out in a world overflowing with content and short attention spans?

The template so far has evolved to a combination of 'push the extreme idea and opinion, dumb it down and communicate in bits and pieces'. The template introduces us to thoughts and ideas, helps reinforce our notions and makes us tribal. It makes our understanding of the world a mile wide and an inch deep. An Instagram reel telling you why buying a house is a waste of money is an example of an opinion prevailing over facts and nuance. The template does not work when the stakes are high.

Crowdsourced information is great if you are looking for a good vegetarian restaurant in Manali or how to tie the Windsor knot. It is not the best way to cure asthma or build a portfolio of investments that delivers your financial goals. Health, physical and financial, is what helps make the best of our talent and the opportunities life gives us.

The old adage 'for health and wealth to be truly enjoyed, there needs to be an interruption' conveys a truth we are indifferent to till there is an interruption. Think of the last time you had diarrhoea. Think of the retired aunt who lost her savings when the co-operative bank that held her high interest deposit went bankrupt. While most physical illnesses are transient and caused by factors

beyond our control, financial stress lasts longer and can often be attributed to our mistakes.

Think of the money you lost because a friend who has 'made millions' in the stock market told you to buy a share that was guaranteed to double in the next two years. Think of the relative who made a high interest yielding deposit with a reputable builder, only to lose the principal when the builder went bust. This book will help you avoid those mistakes.

Yes, what I say in this book I could have said in one hundred and eight Instagram reels or in fifty-one YouTube videos. I chose a book because I don't want you to be distracted by social media algorithms. I want to give you food for thought in quantities that are unsuitable for social media. I hope as you read, you pause and think about what you have read. Ask yourself if what you read makes any sense to you. If you learnt anything new or if it helped you review your thought process.

Your money is one of the most important things in your life. It is the source of your confidence; it gives you identity and it is an important purpose of your life. If everything you read in this book does not help you manage it better, then I have failed as an author.

The book has seven chapters and in each one I have drawn from theories of portfolio management and my own experiences as a wealth manager and investor. I hope the book is worth your time. You may find some of the terms I have used in the book new or technical. There is a glossary at the end of the book that will help you understand these terms.

Writing is an act of hubris. If you are still reading and if you end up reading this book, I owe you my gratitude.

1

*Risk Hai to Ishq Hai**: To Live Is To Dare

Recall the last time you ran and jumped to get on a moving bus or a train. Your brain calculated the 'risk' of injury you were taking and the 'reward' of making it to your destination on time. There was no guarantee that you would be able to get on to the bus or train without seriously injuring yourself.

We all know of instances where people got seriously injured or died while trying to get on to a moving bus or a train, but you took the risk, not waiting for the next bus or train for the 'profit' of making it to your home or office on time and were comfortable with the prospective 'loss' – a serious injury. You took a risk and were rewarded by making it to your destination on time and avoided the loss of injury or time if you had waited for the next bus or train.

The whole decision-making process was intuitive. You did not pick a paper and pen and list down the risks involved and the return you will earn. You saw the train/bus move, realised that you will have to wait for the next one, your brain did the time and motion

---

* The title of the chapter is borrowed from *Scam 1992 – The Harshad Mehta Story. Scam 1992* is a Hindi web series on Sony LIV directed by Hansal Mehta. The dialogue writer is Vaibhav Vishal.

study in fractions and you ran. If you succeeded in catching the train/bus, the risk paid off and you got the return.

Let us take another example of risk and returns from our lives.

Marriage. It is one of the oldest institutions in India and continues to thrive. Someone in the family or you on our own decide now is the time to get married. You either look for a partner or consider if the person you are seeing romantically is the person you want to get married to. You draw up a list of benefits marriage will accrue to you. These benefits range from emotional and financial support, social status and familial comforts. These benefits are the returns you will make by investing time, emotions, financial resources and letting go of the independence that comes from being on our own.

There is no certainty that marriage will make you happy, which is to say there is no guarantee you will get the return you are seeking, defined here as benefits. Marriages are successful – couples are happy and they enjoy the benefits, but there are marriages that end in divorce – couples lose the time, money and the emotions they invested in the marriage.

Getting married, or not getting married, is the process of assessing risk and reward and you will live to see the returns or lack thereof. The decision making involved a combination of data and intuition.

You spoke to people who are or have been married; you have first-hand information from the married life of your parents and you used your instincts to figure out who amongst all the people you met will make you happily married.

Here is a final example of risk and returns assessment from our daily lives before I get to investment portfolios. Like many Indians of my generation, I grew up in a small city and have worked in a metropolis all my life. I decided to let go of the comforts of a small town for my career. The pace of life in a small town is sedate, and my parents had a house I could have continued to live in.

Air quality in Bhopal, the city I grew up in, is excellent and the cost of living is low. I would have had a more enriching life outside of my work. I decided to leave Bhopal because there were no economic opportunities to match my ambitions. I wanted to make money and make it early in my life. I took the risk of toiling in a big city, making money and enjoying an affluent life in a big city.

It came, but at the cost of my health, and my relationships with friends and family. I have to accept the fact that I spent almost all my waking hours working. My story is one of many we see around us.

If you left the town you were born and brought up in for better economic opportunities, you did the same risk reward assessment in your head. You asked if you would risk your health, 'loss' of spare

time in your life and miss out on the returns of familial bonds, for more money.

The three scenarios I have described give us three frameworks of assessing risk and reward in our lives.

You see and you intuitively work out the risk reward framework. You don't need data or advice before you take the plunge. Nobody ever taught you the technique of running after a moving bus, you saw someone do it and next time you needed to figure out the risk-reward of boarding a moving bus, you did not run the numbers in your head. You just ran.

The second scenario – marriage – involves seeking data, soliciting advice from elders or friends, processing them for meaningful information and backing your decision-making process to decide one way or the other.

The third scenario is a combination of the above two. I knew of people who had left Bhopal and built the kind of careers I aspired to. I sought information on career opportunities in metros. How much would those jobs pay and will they make up for the cost of living in a big city? If the money would make up for the comforts of living in my parent's house.

The scenarios and frameworks tell us, all decision-making in life is weighing in on risk vs returns and how we use a combination of what we see, what we know and how we process the information we have. Every decision you make in your life is a Risk Return trade-off. Yes, every decision. The act of reading this book is a risk-return trade-off. You could be watching a movie right now or spending time with your loved ones. You decided to risk your time hoping this book will be useful.

There is no escape from this exercise.

Pause here for a minute and think of the three life-changing decisions you made in your life. The career choices you have made, the person you married, the hobby you gave up on to focus on your career, the job offer you didn't take or the months you spent grinding out a result. What are the decisions whose outcomes you are happy with? Go on, write them down. Write them on the margins of this page. Please do, trust me it will help. Thank you.

As you can see with every decision you made, you took risks. You were rewarded because you took those risks. An indecision or a different decision would have led to a different outcome. Decisions can lead to unexpected outcomes, unanticipated events and disappointments. When you made those decisions, you were aware that they may not lead to desired outcomes. You were confident you would succeed but hand on heart you knew success was not guaranteed.

These unexpected outcomes are a feature of decision making. The chances of unexpected outcomes make all decision making a risky business. Yes, all decision making is risk-taking. Not doing anything is also a decision and like all decisions, not doing anything also carries risks.

A textbook on finance will tell you Risk is the degree of uncertainty of the rate of return on an investment. It will tell you that a loss occurs when the returns do not meet investor expectations. It will also tell you that when the uncertainty is high, investors seek higher returns and when the uncertainty is low, they accept low returns.

In conclusion, every risk is a probability and risk has a direct co-relation with returns. Making an investment is a decision, which makes risk a feature of any investment. Investment risk is one of the risks we face in our life.

The earlier examples would have helped you understand how we assess risk and return in our daily lives and how we can use those frameworks when we invest. All decision making is an assessment of risk and return trade-offs. We accept failure as a cost of decision

making and find ways to maximise our chances of success. Investing is no different.

We have a choice of not investing and avoiding the risk of losing money or we can invest and be rewarded by wealth. Both the decisions – investing and not investing have risks. Skip investing and you lose your money to inflation, while a wrong investment could lead to a loss of the principal. Table 1.1 will help you understand the risks of not investing. It depicts the cost of living in the year 2010 and 2025. I have used a basket of common goods.

Table 1.1: Inflation and Cost of Living

Goods	Price on 1 July 2010 (INR)	Price on 1 July 2025 (INR)
1 Kg Flour	16	54
1 Kg Arhar Dal	79	142
1 Pack of Gold Flake Cigarette, pack of 10	47	100
Rent of a 2 BHK DDA Flat in South Delhi	21,000	45,000
Iphone	35,000	82,900
1 Litre of Petrol in Delhi	52	94.72
1 Ticket at a PVR Theatre in Delhi	100	290
Hero Splendour Bike	49,852	77,103
Maruti Suzuki Swift	5.49 lakh	7.53 lakh
One-way Air Fare: Delhi to Mumbai	6,200	6,800

Note: Data for the table of prices on common goods has been sourced from the internet and from my lived experience in South Delhi. I lived in a rented house in South Delhi from July 2007 to February 2017. The data is for illustrative purposes. Readers are advised to do their primary research for estimating the impact of inflation on their cost of living.

Inflation is a tax on our savings. When you don't invest, you risk the value of your money reducing every year.

Investing comes with its own risks. You can invest in multiple asset classes. Popular asset classes are fixed income, equity, gold and real estate. Table 1.2 shows the value of Rs 1 lakh invested in the Public Provident Fund (PPF), in Nifty 50 Index and in Gold as on 1 July 2010 and 1 July 2025.

Table 1.2: Market Value of Investments

Instrument	1 July 2010	Value as on 1 July 2025
Public Provident Fund	1,00,000	315,230
NSE 50	1,00,000	486,381
Gold	1,00,000	497,056

Figures 1.1 and 1.2 show the daily movement and change in value, of the Nifty 50 Index and Gold over this 15-year period.

Figure 1.1: Movement of NSE Nifty 50 Index

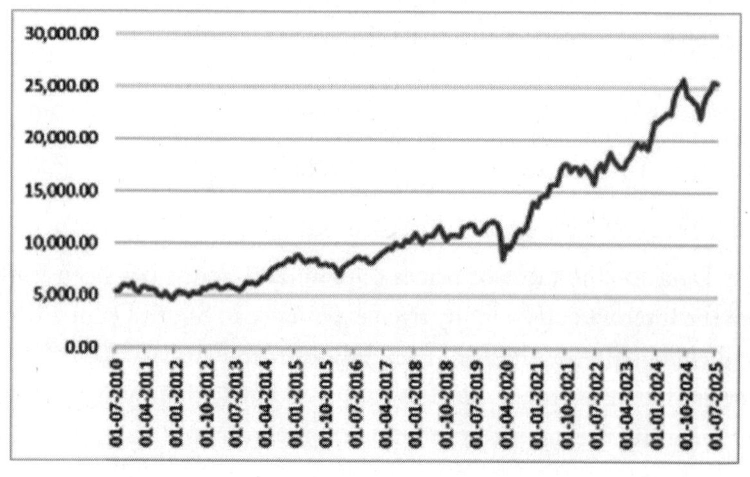

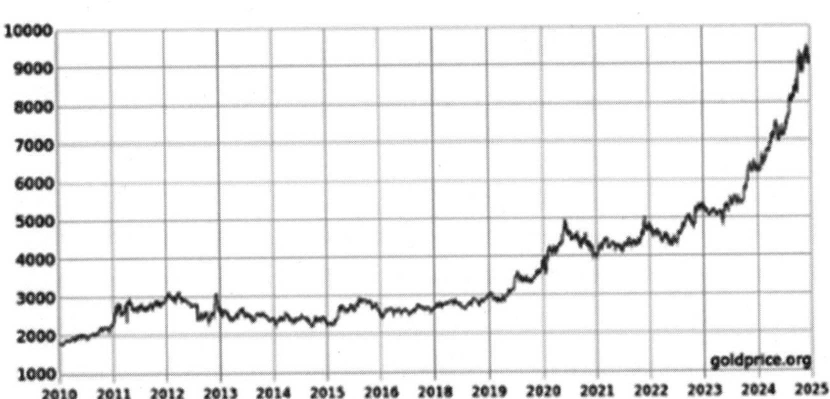

Figure 1.2: Movement of Gold Prices

As you can see, the journey of Rs 1 lakh to Rs 4,86,381 in equity and Rs 4,97,056 in gold was not linear. If you had invested Rs 1 lakh in NSE 50 on 1 January 2011 and sold this investment on 1 January 2012, you would have got Rs 75,381.86 and would have lost Rs 24,618. 14. The same investment, if sold on 2 January 2012, at the price of Rs 75,584.81 would have caused a loss of Rs 24,415.19. If this investment is sold on 1 January 2014 at Rs 102,724.75, it gives a profit of Rs 2,724.75 and if it is sold on 2 January 2014 at Rs 101,412.50, it gives a profit of Rs 1,412.50

The value of the investment fluctuated on a daily basis. The value either went up or came down from the day before. We will call this daily movement in the value of the investment as volatility. It is important that you understand volatility.

The daily price movement is an integral part of equity investments. The value of your investment in listed equity can be found every day. Stock exchanges publish the closing value of equity investments at the end of every trading day. This daily price discovery causes volatility; share prices do not go up every day and when they do go up, they do not go up at the same rate every day.

The investor had to live through this volatility and may have had to exit the investment below Rs 1 lakh if they ended up selling their investment when the value was less than Rs 1 lakh.

This daily change in the value of equity investments is called volatility.

As in life there is no escape from taking risks when it comes to investing. The decision to not invest in asset classes that will beat inflation is a risk. Is there a way we can make the 'risk-return off' work for us?

What can we learn from history! How do investors manage daily ups and downs in the value of their investment and end up making money? Why do elders tell you money is made in property and gold? Why do they say *stock market to satta hai*? How can your savings help you buy your next car, a cottage in the hills, that house with a back garden near a beach and send your daughter for her MBA to an Ivy League college. We will find the answers to these questions in the following chapters.

Summary: Life is a sum total of all the decisions we make. Every decision or indecision is you doing a risk versus return trade-off. The career choices you have made, the person you married or did not marry, the city you live in are all decisions that may or may not have led to desired outcomes. The uncertainty of these outcomes makes all decision making risky. Investing is no different. Every investment decision, even the act of not investing, is a decision, and comes with its own risk. We will learn how to manage this risk and make investing work for us in the following chapters.

2

Diversification
Free Lunch of Risk Management

Peter Bernstein in his book *Against the Gods* writes: 'What separates the modern world from the ancient world is how we understand and manage risk'. The ancients traded and travelled the way we do, albeit at low volumes and a slow pace. They sought prosperity and good health. Ancients had artistic expression and a cultural milieu.

Think of our *Itihaas* (history) – *Mahabharat* and *Ramayan* – and literary works of the Greeks – the *Iliad* and *Odyssey*. Where the ancient world differed from our modern world was in its ability to manage risk. How our ancestors managed risks was different in a very fundamental way – they did not use financial tools to manage risks. The ancients prayed to their gods for health and safety; we continue to pray to our gods for our safety but we also buy insurance!

Our ability to manage risks is one of the wonders of our modern world. The complexity of the modern world makes it riskier than the ancient world. Aeroplanes crash, ships sink, preventable diseases kill millions every year and stock markets crash. The modern world gives us the tools to minimise the impact of these adverse events. We buy insurance to help us reduce the financial burden on the family in case of death and disability. Businesses buy marine insurance to cover for loss of goods in transit. We vaccinate to save ourselves from death and disability; similarly, when we invest in equities, we buy equity derivatives to hedge against a stock market crash.

You may have heard the proverb: Do not keep all your eggs in one basket. This underlines a simple and a powerful tool of risk management as you start to invest and build your portfolio. Legend has it that the early Chinese traders transported goods on the Yangtze River in two boats. In case one sank, some of the goods would make it to the destination. Not keeping all your money in one pocket, a backup of your school essay on the cloud – these are examples of a simple risk management tool we practice.

The tool is common, sensible and so widely used that we don't even think about it. We use it in our everyday life. This tool is called Diversification.

Minimising losses while trying to achieve a desired outcome by trying to achieve the desired end result in multiple ways is called diversification. Let us try and understand this with examples.

An Indian marriage often has one of the families, either the bride or the groom, travel to the other family's city for the wedding ceremonies. The travel involves the transfer of wedding jewellery from one city to another. Families usually entrust the responsibility of carrying the jewellery to multiple members of the family. Their logic is that if one of the family members were to meet with an untoward incident – say, their bag gets stolen – then all the jewellery will not be lost in transit. What does the family achieve in this case? The outcome it wants to achieve. That the jewellery reaches the wedding destination. This they do by entrusting the responsibility of transfer to a number of people. Family members, here, are a proxy for multiple ways.

This is similar to diversification, which is a tool of risk management.

Let us now see how we can use diversification as a tool as we build our portfolio. There are multiple asset classes that we can invest in to achieve our financial goals. For the purpose of this book, we will keep the discussion limited to financial assets.

What do we mean by Financial Assets? A financial asset is an investment that is held in the form of a contract. Investors do not get to hold or take physical custody of the asset. Let's break this down.

Let us start with a universal financial asset – Currency. The Rs 500 note that you have in your wallet is a contract. It is a contract between you and the Government of India; the Reserve Bank of India is a representative of *Bharat Sarkar*. The contract states that

the Government of India owes to the bearer, its assets equal to the value of the currency note. Yes, if you have a note of 500 rupees in your wallet, the Government of India owes you its assets worth Rs 500.

Let us look at a currency note in your wallet. You can see the Governor of the RBI has signed it on behalf of the government and what does he say above his signature? You can exchange this currency note for a deposit with the post office, buy a sovereign gold bond from the government or tender it to buy the new parliament building. The Government of India vide this contract makes this promise to the bearer of the currency note. This promise makes currency a medium of exchange between parties. A currency note, the simplest of financial instruments, is a contract.

Bank fixed deposit is a popular financial asset in India. The certificate of deposit that the bank gives you is a contract. The amount of deposit is the consideration and the interest the bank commits to paying you is the promise. The conditions in the contract are explicit – the amount deposited, tenure of the deposit, the interest rate payable; these are all mentioned and any party that refuses to fulfil its side of the contract has to pay damages. If you decide to foreclose the deposit, that is, withdraw the money from the bank before the end of the tenure of the deposit, you have to pay a penalty and forgo the interest due to you. If the bank refuses to pay interest or the principal amount on the due date, the bank stands to lose its licence and its shareholders stand to lose their capital.

Let us discuss another example of a contract – Equity Investment. Equity investment is when you buy shares in a company. A Share Certificate or Shares held in dematerialised form via a demat account is a contract. When an investor buys a share in a company, the investor enters into a contract. This is a contract between investors and the company. The company form of business is a popular and one of the successful innovations in human history. By definition a company is an 'artificial person'. It is the coming together of individuals. The investor infuses capital in the company to help it grow its business and the company through its agents, the management of the company, promises to share a part of the profits. The management of the company represents the company.

The contract here is different from the contract one enters with the government, via a currency note.

Unlike a contract with the government, a shareholder's contract with the company has risk – the risk that the company may not deliver profits. This risk comes from the nature of business, the competitive environment the company operates in, the ability of its management to use the share capital to deliver profits and the regulatory environment. There is no guarantee that the company will deliver its side of the contract – make profits and share it with the shareholders. The shareholders have no recourse if the company loses their money to unviable businesses or poor execution of strategy. They can enforce their right to change the management and can claim their share on the assets of the company.

A shareholder's contract with the company is like an article of faith. The consideration, the amount shareholders have invested, is known to both the parties to the contract – investor and the management. The promise is not well defined and evolves over a period of time. The contract can be ended by one of the parties – the investor can sell their share without the consent of the company. The management of the company does not have the right to end the contract.

The peculiar nature of the contract, where one side pays the consideration while the other side is not obligated to deliver on the promise, makes the contract uncertain and the investors expect to be compensated for this uncertainty in the contract. This uncertainty is the risk they take.

Shareholders of a company expect returns on their investments in excess of returns they would get on a bank fixed deposit or a Government of India bond, as compensation for this risk. This is an important aspect of equity investing. Let us discuss this in detail.

You open an account with a stock broker and buy 500 shares of, let's say, State Bank of India. You are now an investor in the company and have entered into a contract with the bank. The agents of the bank – its management – represent the bank in this contract. The management of the company – its CEO, all the Chief

General Managers, its General Managers all the way down to the Branch Manager of your nearest SBI branch – is now party to this contract. They are supposed to work in a way that the value of your shares goes up. You have no control over how the bank staff goes about its work.

As an outsider you don't understand how the bank decides who it gives loans to and how it ensures that the loans are repaid. You don't understand how they decide on the rate of interest they offer on deposits. You are not aware of how they manage various technology platforms and their costs.

At the end of every three months, the management publishes its accounts and if you know how to read a bank's balance sheet you can try and get an idea of what the management is doing to keep its side of the contract, but if you don't know how to read the balance sheet you are clueless.

The surest way to know if the management is keeping its promise is the price of the share. If the price of the State Bank of India stock goes up then you can say that the management is fulfilling the promise. The shares are traded on the stock exchange and those who understand the balance sheet and workings of SBI will buy more shares. This increase in demand for shares will increase the share price. Similarly, when those who understand the balance sheet and working of SBI decide that the management is not growing the bank's profits, that is to say that it is not keeping its part of the contract, they will sell the shares. This will reduce the demand for shares and the price will go down.

It is because you don't know what the management is doing on a daily basis and you cannot force them to deliver on their promise. Remember the promise is never clearly laid out that you demand a return higher than what SBI gives you on its fixed deposits. We have discussed factors that SBI management can influence; the bank operates in an economy and a business environment that has variables beyond its control. SBI and its management have to follow regular changes in rules and regulations.

Like you, no SBI manager was prepared for Demonetisation or Covid-induced lockdown. The company and its management operate in a dynamic environment. It is one of the reasons the contract is not explicit on their promise.

It is this 'unfair' nature of the contract – a party that has paid the consideration and now awaits the delivery of the promise – that makes it lucrative. The consideration amount, if the management executes the business strategy, is returned manifolds and the returns continue to accrue over years. It is important to understand how this contract works.

Investors tend to see past returns from equity investments and decide, on the basis of these returns, their allocation in this asset class. They overlook that past is past. Just because the management of the company has delivered profits and the share price has gone up in the past does not mean that it will continue to deliver profits and share price will continue to go up. There is no guarantee that the management of the company will continue to deliver on its promise.

Investors forget that the delivery of the promise in the past keeps the ambiguity of the contract intact. If the price of SBI stock has gone up in the last one or three or five years does not mean it will continue to go up in the next one, three or five years. There are no guarantees that the management of the bank will continue to deliver on its promise in the future, just because it has delivered on its promise in the past. The uncertainty and ambiguity of the promise make the contract risky. This uncertainty is the justification for the higher returns investors expect when they enter into the contract. It is important for investors to understand that they get higher returns because of this risk.

The corollary of this aspect of the contract is that if an investor gets high returns, they carry high risk in the portfolio. If the share price of a company continues to go up at a high rate every month, investors should conclude that the risk in the investment is also growing month on month.

Every investment in equity adds risk to the portfolio. Risk of not only the management failing to deliver on the returns but also the risk of the management losing the amount investors have given to the company.

Let us now consider another financial contract – the asset in this contract is one of the oldest assets and has universal acceptance – Gold. Yes, as an investor you can buy gold as a financial instrument.

You can buy units of mutual funds that have invested in gold, invest in gold exchange traded funds or purchase sovereign gold bonds issued by the Government of India.

The way these contracts work is simple. One party keeps the physical custody of gold, and offers this physical quantity in exchange for money. The consideration is paid by the investor and the custodian of the gold promises to mark the value of this consideration with the market price of gold. Let us see how this contract works with the example of the Government of India issued sovereign gold bonds.

The Government of India issues sovereign gold bonds as an alternative to buying physical gold in India. Investors get a bond and the value of this bond matches the price of gold. The duration of this bond is eight years. At the time of the bond's issue, the government states the price of one gram of gold. Investors can buy any quantity from one gram to 20 kilograms. The government promises to buy back these bonds from the investors, at the end of the eight years at the market price of gold.

The first of these bonds were issued in the year 2015 and the maturity proceeds were paid out in the year 2023. The value of the contract was determined by the price of gold. Investors in the first tranche paid a consideration amount of Rs 2,684 for a gram of gold and were paid back Rs 6,116 for a gram at the end of the contract period.

This contract is different from the three contracts discussed earlier – currency, bank fixed deposit and equity investment. The currency contract defines consideration, promise and its value is explicit and its duration does not impact its value. It is a low risk contract an investor enters with the sovereign. A fixed deposit is a contract with a consideration, promise, duration and can be valued any time – both the parties know the cost of breaking the contract. Equity investing/share purchase is a contract with a defined consideration and an uncertain promise. The value of the contract fluctuates.

A sovereign gold bond has a defined consideration, promise and duration but its value is contingent on the movement of gold prices. The investor, at the time of investing, knows the price of gold, she also knows when her money will be returned but does not know the value at the time of maturity. This amount will be decided by the price of the gold when the bond matures. The bond is a fixed duration contract with stated consideration and promise but the value of the promise is uncertain.

A contract like this should compensate the investor with a higher return than a fixed income contract with the sovereign. A fixed income contract with the government can be entered into by buying a government-issued interest paying bond. A sovereign gold bond carries no guarantee of the price at which it will mature. Investors can demand compensation for this uncertainty. They are not compensated by the government because the consideration in the contract is paid for a commodity whose price is determined by the market.

How is the price of gold determined by the markets? Gold is one of the oldest asset classes and its acceptance is universal. There is no economic activity that influences the price of gold. Production of food grains, steel manufacturing and extension of credit line for a business has no relation to the price of gold. Gold prices go up because of its universal acceptance as a store of value and a medium of exchange.

Let us try and understand universal acceptance. Suppose you have a business of manufacturing agricultural goods. You have a query from Botswana for an order of Rs 10 lakh. The buyer says he will pay in Botswana Pula – his currency. You are not confident of the value of Botswana Pula and would rather be paid in Indian rupees. There are two ways of doing this transaction.

The usual way is to do the trade in US dollars or you can promise the buyer to accept payment in gold.

The buyer knows the rate at which he will be able to procure gold worth Rs 10 lakh in Botswana and you know you will be able to sell that gold in India for Rs 10 lakh. Yes, it is a complicated way of doing a business transaction and there will be challenges of exchanging physical gold. The point here is that the buyer in Botswana understands and accepts gold as a store of value and a medium of exchange like you do.

The value of gold changes based on what the buyers and sellers think is the price at which they decide to exchange it. Its universal acceptance makes its price sensitive to its global demand and supply. Every individual on this planet accepts gold as a medium of exchange and considers it valuable. You can buy gold in Dubai and you will be able to sell it in Manhattan, Mumbai and Madagascar.

Historically the price of gold has outgrown the rate of inflation. *Sona mehnga ho gaya hai* – they say in Hindi speaking parts of India. What they mean is inflation. Gold delivers returns that exceed the rate of inflation in the economy. Here we must note that gold prices do not increase in linear fashion. Refer to Figure 1.2 which shows gold price movement from 1 July 2010 till 1 July 2025.

As you can see, gold prices have peaks and bottoms. Unlike a bank deposit, gold does not deliver time-bound and fixed returns. This fluctuation and uncertain nature of gold prices make investment in gold and sovereign gold bonds unique. The consideration and promise are explicit but the payoff is uncertain.

We have now discussed the four asset classes that as an investor you can invest in as you try and achieve your financial goals. (1) Currency – holding hard cash; (2) ICICI Prudential Short-Term Debt fund – a mutual fund scheme that invests in fixed income instruments; (3) Equities – share in a business and (4) Gold.

I have considered ICICI Prudential Short-Term Fund as a proxy for a bank deposit.

Table 2.1 shows us the returns these four asset classes have delivered in the last 15 years.

Table 2.1: Market Value of Investments and Compounded Annual Growth Rate (CAGR)

Asset Class	1 July 2010	1 July 2025	CAGR
Liquid Cash	100,000.00	100,000.00	0.00%
ICICI Prudential Short Term Fund	100,000.00	311,421.36	7.87%
Nifty 50	100,000.00	486,380.77	11.12%
Gold	100,000.00	497,056.38	11.28%

As we size up the returns that these asset classes have delivered, let us revisit a variable that will influence our financial goals. Inflation – *Mehangai.*

An economics textbook will tell you that inflation is too much money chasing too few goods and services. In other words, when demand for a commodity is more than its supply, the price of the commodity goes up. To understand how this plays out in real life, refer to Table 1.1 in Chapter 1. Have a look at how the prices of goods have increased.

Inflation is as certain in India as change in seasons. There is no escaping inflation. Our ability to buy goods for a given sum of money has diminished every year since we started keeping records in India.

We now understand inflation.

Let us now look at the idea of real return. Real return is the return an investment generates adjusted for inflation. If the bank offers you a 7% interest rate on your one-year fixed deposit and in the same year the rate of inflation is 7%, then your real return is zero. The maturity amount of your deposit is Rs 107 but the goods that you could buy for Rs 100 a year ago now cost Rs 107. See your money hasn't grown in real terms. Although your Rs 100 has grown to Rs 107, you cannot buy more of the goods that you could buy a year ago. Your money has seen nominal growth, not real growth.

If we have to achieve our financial goals, it is important that money grows in real terms. The car you are dreaming of buying in three years will cost more in three years than it does today. Your children's college education will cost more than what your college education cost your parents. The house you are planning to buy will get expensive. Unless an investment delivers a return higher than the rate of inflation, it will not help achieve financial goals. The Government of India records tell us that average annual inflation has been 6.5% since 2010.

Table 2.2 gives us the real returns delivered since 2010 by the four asset classes that we have discussed. The values are in INR.

Table 2.2: Nominal and Real Returns on Investments

Asset Class	1 July 2010	1 July 2025	CAGR	Real Returns
Liquid Cash	100,000.00	100,000.00	0.00%	-6.50%
ICICI Prudential Short Term Fund	100,000.00	311,421.36	7.87%	1.37%
Nifty 50	100,000.00	486,380.77	11.12%	4.62%
Gold	100,000.00	497,056.38	11.28%	4.78%

Rate of inflation is 6.5%. Average consumer price index (CPI) since 2010 has been 6.5%.

Equity and gold have delivered high real returns amongst these four asset classes. So should the investor put all her money in equity and be assured that her financial goals will be met? Alas, life is not that simple.

Refer to Figures 1.1 and 1.2 in Chapter 1. We see that equities have given a 11.12% annual return for the last 15 years but they have not given a 11.57% annual return every year. Equity and gold have delivered real returns but the time period over which they will deliver these returns is unpredictable and impossible to gauge. The unpredictable nature of these returns has an implication on your financial plan. As the returns over a given period of time are unpredictable, investors cannot time their cash outflows to their capital gains from equities and gold.

Before we proceed, I would like you to note my bias for equities. An investment in equities is an investment in economic activity. Capital is invested in businesses that deliver returns out of their profits. An investment in gold is an investment in the 'demand versus supply' dynamic of a universal commodity. This book carries the author's bias and considers that equities give investors their best chance at meeting their financial goals.

Let us get back to cash outflows and capital gains. Assume you would like to buy a car. You decide that you would like to own a car worth Rs 5 lakh five years from now. You see that the NSE Nifty 50 has delivered a return of 11.12% over 15 years, so you decide to invest Rs 2.5 lakh in the index today and wait for this investment to turn into Rs 4.9 lakh in five years' time.

Table 2.3 shows five-year returns of investment in Nifty 50 funds for various investment dates since 2009. We have taken 1 January, 1 April, 1 July and 1 December as our date of investment. To expand our sample size, we have also taken the dates of Diwali trade, 25 January, 14 August and 1 October (stock markets are closed on national holidays). To round up our sample to 10 days, we have also taken two other dates.

As you can see from the table, the 15-year compound annual growth rate (CAGR) has ranged from 14.84% to 10.62%. However, there are multiple five-year time periods when NSE 50 has delivered single-digit five-year CAGR. If you had invested on 1 December 2014, your portfolio would have grown at 8% CAGR till 1 December 2019. If you had invested on the day of Diwali in 2019 your portfolio would have grown by 15.79% till Diwali in 2024. You can choose your own date on the website and see five-year rolling returns on NSE 50. Note that these are past returns.

As you plan for the future you have to consider risks that may impact returns on your equity portfolio. Data shows that investors

Table 2.3: Five-Year Returns of NSE Nifty 50 Index

Year	1 Jan	1 April	1 July	1 Dec	14 Aug	25 Jan	1 Oct	Diwali Trade	16 Nov	23 May
2009	14.96%	14.03%	10.74%	9.75%	11.21%	18.53%	12.05%	9.28%	10.65%	11.69%
2010	12.53%	9.16%	10.20%	5.31%	9.34%	12.03%	5.73%	4.39%	5.44%	11.40%
2011	6.56%	6.14%	9.52%	12.10%	11.32%	5.30%	10.12%	10.64%	10.03%	7.49%
2012	10.49%	12.13%	14.02%	12.40%	12.73%	10.58%	12.96%	12.36%	12.88%	14.18%
2013	12.81%	12.61%	14.61%	11.50%	14.77%	12.99%	10.52%	10.88%	12.02%	11.82%
2014	12.21%	11.90%	7.56%	8.00%	7.20%	11.60%	7.37%	7.73%	7.23%	9.61%
2015	6.31%	3.80%	5.35%	11.96%	5.59%	6.75%	7.93%	10.31%	10.36%	1.34%
2016	12.51%	13.26%	12.78%	16.22%	13.77%	13.87%	15.42%	15.74%	17.28%	14.44%
2017	15.16%	12.95%	11.23%	11.45%	12.56%	15.31%	11.75%	11.81%	12.50%	11.55%
2018	9.88%	10.96%	11.71%	14.88%	11.19%	10.05%	12.93%	13.00%	13.10%	11.96%
2019	14.94%	13.98%	17.55%	14.21%	16.96%	14.50%	15.30%	15.79%	14.62%	14.53%
15 yr CAGR	**14.43%**	**13.30%**	**11.87%**	**10.62%**	**11.72%**	**14.84%**	**11.53%**	**10.88%**	**10.79%**	**11.92%**

 DIVERSIFICATION

cannot invest only in equities and be assured their financial goals will be met. If they stay invested for periods of five years and above, they will get real returns but there is no guarantee that the returns will match their cash outflows. Cash outflow means the date on which investors will need the money to meet their expenses. The value of their investments could be lower when they need the money.

So here we are; an asset class that delivers real returns delivers, them in an unpredictable fashion and the asset class where the returns are predictable and can be timed (fixed income) does not deliver real returns. What is the way out? We go back to where we started. Diversification.

An investor has financial goals that span various time spans. You may have a financial goal that is one to two years away and a financial goal that is 10 years away. Remember a financial goal that is 10 years away, will be two years away in eight years from now. As an investor you must know how to match the tenure of your financial goals with the asset class you invest in and review the time horizon in which you plan to achieve your financial goals.

To summarise, each financial asset is a contract. The returns these contracts generate are dependent on the ability of the promisor to deliver on his side of the contract. Returns and timelines over which these returns will be delivered are predictable in currency and fixed income contracts and uncertain in equity and gold contracts. This brings us to the conclusion that investors need a combination of assets in their portfolio. What is this combination and how can they ensure that the combination helps them meet their financial goal? We will discuss this in the next chapter.

Summary: You can achieve your financial goals by investing in financial assets. Each financial asset is a contract. When you invest in a financial asset, you enter into a contract. The risks in each of these contracts are different. The varied nature of risks leads to

differences in returns that these investments deliver. You need real returns from your investments to meet your financial goals. The best way to earn real returns and meet your financial goals is to invest in a variety of financial assets.

Note: The return generated by ICICI Prudential Short Term Debt Fund has been calculated on the basis of public information. The data for these calculations has not been sourced from the ICICI Prudential Asset Management company. It is for illustrative purposes only and should not be considered investment advice. Readers are advised to do their own due diligence.

3

Discipline of Asset Allocation

In the previous chapter we discussed the returns that various financial assets deliver. We learnt some asset classes have predictable returns – at the time of investment we know the period over which they will deliver these returns. A bank fixed deposit is an example of such an investment. On the day the deposit is booked, the depositor knows the duration of the deposit, the interest they will earn during the tenure of the deposit and also the maturity amount at the end of the tenure.

There are asset classes – equities – where we have historical data on the returns they generated across various spans and we can invest hoping similar returns will be generated in the future. This hope is the risk we carry and the return the investors get is the reward for this risk.

We also discovered that not all investments deliver real returns. Real return is the return an investment generates over and above the rate of inflation. To achieve our financial goals, we need to invest in assets that deliver real returns but the asset class with a long history of delivering real returns (equities) has unpredictable and non-linear returns. How do we then make a portfolio of investments that helps us achieve our financial goals?

We practice the Discipline of Asset Allocation.

If there is one takeaway for you in this book, I hope it is the discipline of asset allocation. What you will read next will sound hyperbole but it is as true as Monday follows Sunday. THE SINGLE BIGGEST REASON FOR PEOPLE FAILING TO MEET THEIR FINANCIAL GOALS, DESPITE INVESTING IN ALL ASSET CLASSES FOR ALL SORTS OF TIME DURATIONS, IS THEIR FAILURE TO PRACTISE THE DISCIPLINE OF ASSET ALLOCATION.

Let us now discuss the concept of asset allocation in detail and then we will see how that discipline will help you achieve your financial goals.

Take a pen and paper or open a spreadsheet. Make a list of your financial goals. Some of these goals could be buying a new car, going for studies abroad, accumulating capital for starting your own business, building a corpus for children's education, a romantic trip to Europe or retirement fund.

Stop reading right now; get a pen and paper or open the spreadsheet and do it now. Recording your financial goals is the first step. If you don't do this your plan will fail. Any ask that is not recorded is not a serious ask. Anything that is not recorded cannot be measured. Anything that cannot be measured cannot be tracked and anything that is not tracked either stays incomplete or fails to deliver desired outcomes. So if you are still reading this without a pen and a paper or an open spreadsheet you are taking the first misstep. You have spent your hard-earned money on buying this book and have spent precious time reading it. Both of these are serious investments, so let's start making a return on these investments.

Record your top five financial goals. Thank you.

Now that you have recorded your top five financial goals, write down the date on which you want these goals achieved. This need not be a specific date. It can be a month, two years, three years, five years, whatever is the time horizon you have in mind. Now you have a list of your financial goals and the time horizon over which you would like to achieve these goals.

Before we move ahead, please make a note of an important variable, time. While your financial goals can be considered stock, time is a flow. A financial goal that is five years away, will be four years from now one year away. This is an often-overlooked aspect when we invest to meet our financial goals. While we keep a track of the value of our investments, we tend to lose sight of the time horizon. This has serious implications. Reconciliation of time with the goal and the asset class suitable for that time duration is the key to achieving financial goals.

Let us try and understand this with an example. Simran is a mother of a 10-year-old and wants to plan for his college education. The first milestone, when she expects an outflow of cash, is eight years away, when her son will turn 18. Considering the time horizon she has, Simran starts investing in equities via the equity mutual fund route. She figures out she will need a sum of Rs 50 lakh, assumes that her equity portfolio will deliver an annual compounded return of 13%.

She decides to invest in equity mutual funds via the Systematic Investment Plan (SIP) method. An SIP is a method wherein the investor invests a pre-decided amount, on a pre-decided date for a pre-decided duration. The SIP calculator tells her that she needs to invest Rs 30,600 a month and her financial goal will be achieved. Seven years from the month she starts investing, her invested amount will be Rs 25.7 lakh and its market value will be Rs 40.84 lakh. Yes, that Rs 40.84 lakh will become Rs 50 lakh in the next year. This will happen because she will add another 3.67 lakh in the next one year and the magic of compounding will do the rest. But at the end of seven years, her corpus is 40.84 lakh and she is one year away from her goal.

Refer to Table 2.3 and our discussion on returns of Nifty 50 since 2009 in the previous chapter. There were multiple years when the one-year return was negative or below 13%. Life and stock market being what they are, there is no guarantee, the next year will be favourable for Simran. If the equity market is down by 10% in the next one year, her corpus will be 40.06 lakh at the end of eight years; remember she will continue with her SIP and invest 3.67 lakh in the year.

A 10% correction in the markets will take her corpus down to 40.05 lakh. Eight years of disciplined investing and Simran is still short of her financial goal by a whopping 25%. If this scenario sounds like a particular case of bad luck, let's look at some data. The graphs below capture Nifty returns for the next one year from every day in the years 2015 and in the year 2021.

Figure 3.1: Movement of NSE Nifty 50 Index, 2015

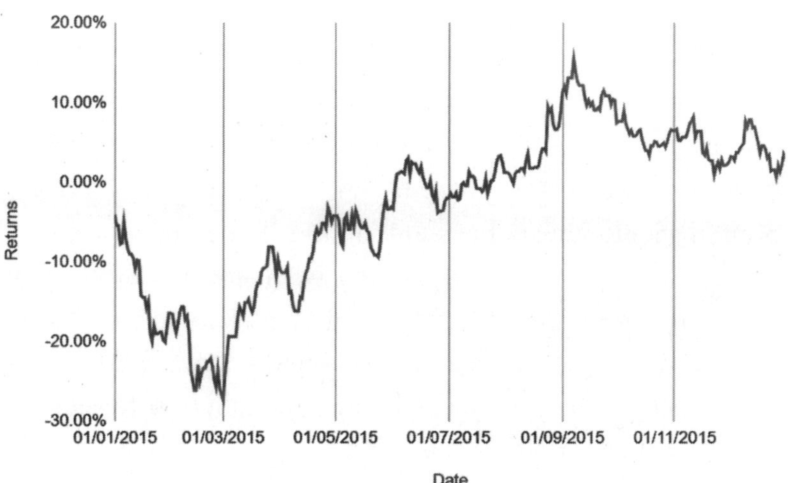

I have chosen these two years, from the last 11 years, because these are the years where Nifty has generated the lowest and the highest return for a calendar year.

The data above tells us that equity markets can deliver below their long-term returns over a one-year period. Nobody knows where the stock market will be in a year's time. No, not even

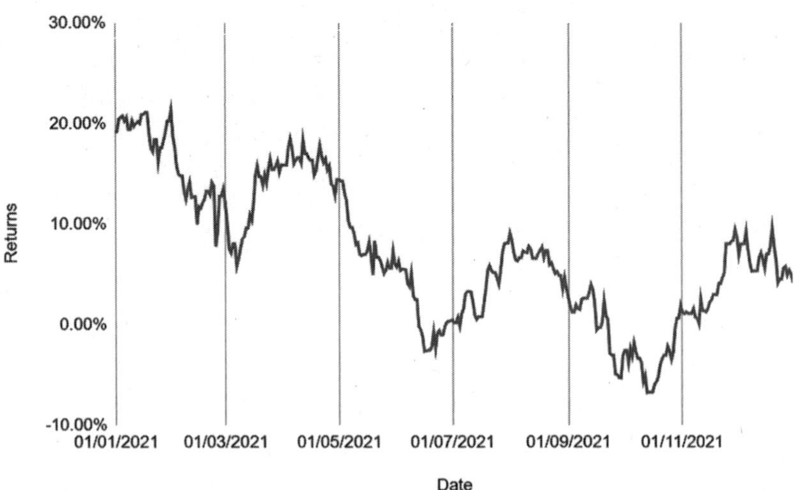

Warren Buffet knows that. Years of savings and investments in the right asset class can fail if we do not stick to the discipline of asset allocation. What should Simran do? How can she ensure that her financial goals are met?

Simran should rework her sums and break the time duration of her financial goals in two parts. Part 1 when she will invest in an asset class that gives high real returns like equities and part 2 when she will move the corpus she has accumulated to a fixed income portfolio and preserve her capital. The time duration for equities can be seven years. During this period, she should have invested in Rs 35000 in equity mutual funds via a monthly SIP. At the end of seven years, her amount invested would be Rs 29.4 lakh and the market value of the corpus will be Rs 46.72 lakh. This money invested in a fixed income instrument that gives an annual return of 7% would take her corpus to Rs 50 lakh in eight years. Sounds simple, doesn't it?

Well, Yes and No. The thumb rule to consider here is that do not stay invested in equities if your investment horizon is one year away. What makes following this thumb rule difficult is the investor's ability to save that incremental amount, a difference of 4400 a month, could be too high for Simran to start with. As her income grows, she may be able to afford it but to start with, investors start with what they can afford. The answer is not in staying invested in equities when your financial goal is one year away. The answer lies in finding a way to invest more. Alternatively, she could look at generating a return that is higher than 13%.

The following can help you decide the time duration for various investment options.

- 0–1 Year   Fixed Income Instruments
- 1–3 Years   Hybrid/ Dynamic Asset Allocation Based Mutual Funds
- 3–5 Years   Large Cap/Flexicap/Multicap Equity Mutual Funds
- 5 Yrs and above   Mid Cap/Small Cap-based Equity Mutual Funds and Gold

We now go back to the goal sheet we had prepared when you started reading this chapter. Against the list of financial goals, you can now allocate the investment option and decide on your portfolio's asset allocation. You can follow what you have just read and call it the 'Time to Goal' asset allocation model and it will help you achieve your goals.

We now move on to another model of asset allocation model that helps investors achieve their financial goals. We call this fixed asset allocation. This approach is different from investment-horizon-based asset allocation. The amount you invest in a particular asset class and how long you stay invested in that asset class is not a factor in determining your asset allocation. Your asset allocation is decided by what percentage of your portfolio you would like to allocate in growth assets and what percentage of your portfolio you would like to have in low risk/fixed income assets.

Let us try and understand this approach with how Simran can construct her portfolio in the fixed asset allocation model. As a working woman with a regular source of income, Simran decides she can afford high risk and volatility in her portfolio if that results in high real returns. She decides to allocate 70% of her portfolio to equities and retains 30% of her portfolio in fixed income instruments.

Table 3.1: Market Value of Fixed Allocation Portfolio

Date	Equity (in INR)	Fixed Income (INR)	Total (INR)	Equity Allocation	Fixed Income
01/01/2008	700,000.00	300,000.00	1,000,000.00	70.00%	30.00%
31/12/2008	345,588.22	348,659.40	694,247.62	49.78%	50.22%
31/12/2009	596,082.58	368,946.72	965,029.30	61.77%	38.23%
31/12/2010	701,509.52	385,010.45	1,086,519.96	64.56%	35.44%
31/12/2011	528,245.46	418,550.35	946,795.81	55.79%	44.21%
31/12/2012	677,955.36	458,500.07	1,136,455.42	59.66%	40.34%
31/12/2013	717,920.53	491,681.47	1,209,602.00	59.35%	40.65%
31/12/2014	943,761.34	548,478.52	1,492,239.86	63.24%	36.76%
31/12/2015	907,213.94	592,307.04	1,499,520.98	60.50%	39.50%
31/12/2016	931,856.10	658,234.95	1,590,091.04	58.60%	41.40%
31/12/2017	1,188,878.40	697,101.35	1,885,979.75	63.04%	36.96%
31/12/2018	1,242,941.89	737,860.13	1,980,802.02	62.75%	37.25%
31/12/2019	1,597,068.85	809,204.65	2,406,273.50	66.37%	33.63%
31/12/2020	2,008,022.00	895,365.03	2,903,387.03	69.16%	30.84%
31/12/2021	2,073,159.08	930,078.36	3,003,237.44	69.03%	30.97%
31/12/2022	1,982,086.80	1,045,462.98	3,027,549.77	65.47%	34.53%
CAGR			**7.66%**		

 DISCIPLINE OF ASSET ALLOCATION

Let us say she starts her portfolio with an investment of Rs 10 lakh on 1 January 2008. For the purposes of this exercise, we will assume that she invested 70% of her corpus in NSE Nifty 50 Index and 30% of her corpus in ICICI Prudential short term debt fund.

Table 3.1 shows the value of her portfolio at the end of every year till 2022.

We discover that as the value of her portfolio changes, her asset allocation changes too. She ends up with a corpus of Rs 30.27 lakh at a CAGR of 7.66% over a 15-year period. There are points when her equity allocation is above and below 70%. As she did not rebalance her portfolio, add to equity when allocation went below 70% and book profits when it went above 70%, the value of her portfolio at the end of 15 years stood at 30.27 lakh.

What if she had rebalanced her portfolio? Keeping her asset allocation constant. 70% in equities and 30% in fixed income. What would be the value of her portfolio at the end of 15 years?

To understand the concept of dynamic asset allocation, we don't need Simran to be invested in a hypothetical portfolio. In India asset managers offer mutual funds schemes that have multiple asset classes as their underlying investments. These mutual fund schemes are called Multi Asset Allocation Funds. Fund managers manage the allocation across these asset classes dynamically.

They have in-house models that decide how much they should allocate to equity, what should be the allocation in fixed income and what should be the allocation in commodities. As the prices of these asset classes move, sometimes in tandem and sometimes with the correlation of their price movements being negative, the fund managers rebalance asset allocation.

Multi Asset Allocation funds in India, also have regulatory compulsions. Fund managers of these schemes have to maintain minimum levels of allocation in individual asset classes. The oldest Multi Asset Allocation in India is managed by ICICI Prudential Asset Management Company. The scheme is called ICICI

Prudential Multi Asset Allocation Fund. The fund has been in existence for over twenty years now.

Table 3.2 shows the calendar year returns of the scheme for a 20 years period.

Table 3.2: Annual Returns of ICICI Prudential Multi Asset Allocation Fund. Date of Investment – 1 January 2005

Year	ICICI MAA
2005	58.54%
2006	58.31%
2007	42.15%
2008	-44.05%
2009	75.83%
2010	21.26%
2011	-20.31%
2012	31.65%
2013	15.59%
2014	37.10%
2015	-1.10%
2016	11.90%
2017	27.81%
2018	-1.77%
2019	7.79%
2020	10.11%
2021	34.22%
2022	16.84%
2023	24.33%
2024	16.42%
CAGR	**17.80%**

The fund has delivered a CAGR of 17.80% in this 20-year period. A 17.80% CAGR means an annual return of 17.80% compounded over a 20-year period.

Table 3.3 shows the calendar year returns of BSE 500 for the same 20 years. BSE 500 is a broad index published by Bombay Stock Exchange; it captures growth in the stock prices of India's top 500 listed companies.

Table 3.3: Annual Returns of BSE 500 Index.
Date of Investment – 1 January 2005

Year	BSE 500
2005	39.23%
2006	38.85%
2007	63.02%
2008	-58.14%
2009	90.23%
2010	16.35%
2011	-27.41%
2012	31.20%
2013	3.25%
2014	36.96%
2015	-0.82%
2016	3.78%
2017	35.94%
2018	-3.08%
2019	7.75%
2020	16.80%
2021	30.11%
2022	3.34%
2023	24.85%
2024	14.55%
CAGR	**13.64%**

The index has delivered a CAGR of 13.47% in this 20-year period. This means that an investment in a BSE 500 index fund would have delivered a 13.47% annual return, compounded annually.

In the last twenty-two years, the stock markets have grown in lock and step with the growth of the Indian economy. Why am I comparing the returns of a Multi Asset Portfolio with a pure equity portfolio? I will answer the question before the end of this chapter.

The National Stock Exchange of India (NSE) has indices that track the stock price movements of India's top 500 companies arranged in the descending order of their market capitalisation. The top 100 companies fall under the Nifty 100 Index, the next 150 fall under the Nifty Mid Cap 150 Index and the next 250 fall under the Nifty 250 Small Cap Index.

These indices also have track records going back years. Table 3.4 captures the value of Rs 1 lakh invested in a large cap mutual fund scheme, a mid-cap mutual fund scheme and a small cap fund scheme on 1 January 2008, on 31 December of 2008 and every subsequent year.

Table 3.4: Market Value of Rs 1 Lakh Invested in Nifty 100, Nifty 150 Mid Cap and Nifty 250 Small Cap Index

Year	NIFTY 100	NIFTY Mid Cap 150	NIFTY Small Cap 250
2008	46,189	33,887	30,332
2009	84,396	71,351	64,886
2010	99,513	84,549	75,432
2011	73,831	57,415	48,252
2012	96,425	82,839	66,677
2013	102,657	80,343	61,250

Year	NIFTY 100	NIFTY Mid Cap 150	NIFTY Small Cap 250
2014	136,709	128,755	103,861
2015	133,419	139,578	114,460
2016	138,227	147,124	114,875
2017	181,145	227,078	180,672
2018	183,206	196,812	132,250
2019	202,295	196,263	121,309
2020	232,356	244,114	151,748
2021	290,533	358,385	245,746
2022	301,086	369,009	236,786
2023	361,440	530,180	350,670
2024	403,930	656,357	443,347
CAGR	8.559%	11.70%	9.16%

What does this data tell us? Before we move ahead, let us discuss the concept of drawdown. The term drawdown in the portfolio means the decrease in the market value of the investment. Let us try and understand this with an example.

Kabir Narayanan invests Rs 10,000 in a mutual fund. This is an investment in an equity mutual fund and its market value changes with the changes in the value of underlying stocks that the portfolio holds. The value of the underlying stocks declines by 10%. This results in the mark to market value of Kabir's investment dropping to Rs 9000.

The difference between the amount invested and the market value, when the market value is less than the amount invested is called drawdown. The term drawdown is also used when the value of the portfolio has gone down below its previous high. Please note if Kabir does not redeem his investment, he has not incurred a loss; the portfolio is negative or has a drawdown. This is a notional loss; it is only if he redeems the investment that he will incur a real loss. Drawdown is the decline in market value of the investment.

Refer to the Figure 1.1, on the movement of Nifty NSE 50 Index in Chapter 1. The movement is not linear; stock markets see daily change in prices and rarely do we see markets moving in any one direction for extended periods.

Drawdown, since it is measured from the last mark to market value of the investment, is a feature of any portfolio. Let us assume that the Rs 10,000 that Kabir invested becomes worth Rs 14,000 in four years. At the end of the fifth year, the value of that investment is Rs 13,500. This means that in the fifth year, Kabir's portfolio has seen a drawdown of 3.57%. The drawdowns in the portfolio are what we mean when we say a portfolio is volatile. The extent of this volatility should be considered by investors when they decide on which asset to invest in.

Historically, portfolios with only equity as the underlying investment have demonstrated far more volatility than a fixed income portfolio. Let us take a look at Table 3.5 to understand drawdowns.

Table 3.5: Market Value and Drawdowns of Rs 10 Lakh Invested in ICICI Multi Asset Allocation Fund and BSE 500 Index on 1 January 2005

Year	ICICI MAA	BSE 500	ICICI Drawdown	BSE 500 Drawdown
31/12/2005	1,585,430.97	1,392,251.58		
31/12/2006	2,509,916.09	1,933,166.82		
31/12/2007	3,567,887.11	3,151,462.14		

Year	ICICI MAA	BSE 500	ICICI Drawdown	BSE 500 Drawdown
31/12/2008	1,996,186.12	1,319,223.62	-44.05%	-58.14%
31/12/2009	3,509,916.09	2,509,545.24		
31/12/2010	4,256,292.91	2,919,893.34		
31/12/2011	3,391,685.74	2,119,457.62	-20.31%	-27.41%
31/12/2012	4,465,293.67	2,780,707.06		
31/12/2013	5,161,327.23	2,871,215.37		
31/12/2014	7,076,277.65	3,932,389.26		
31/12/2015	6,998,474.45	3,900,333.40	-1.10%	-0.82%
31/12/2016	7,831,045.00	4,047,856.40		
31/12/2017	10,009,153.32	5,502,580.24		
31/12/2018	9,832,189.17	5,333,006.91	-1.77%	-3.08%
31/12/2019	10,597,635.39	5,746,377.21		
31/12/2020	11,669,336.38	6,711,963.00		
31/12/2021	15,662,471.40	8,733,206.43		
31/12/2022	18,300,533.94	9,024,709.42		
31/12/2023	22,752,860.41	11,267,336.39		
31/12/2024	26,488,558.35	12,906,348.46		
CAGR	**17.80%**	**13.64%**		

The changes in the value of these portfolios capture the drawdowns of these portfolios.

As you can see, the fund has delivered higher returns in the last 20 years than the BSE 500 and the drawdowns it has seen are lesser than the drawdowns of the pure equity portfolio. Why is it important to consider volatility in the portfolio? Recall we invest to meet our financial goals. The asset class that gives the highest real return is prone to higher drawdowns. This makes it difficult to match our cash outflows with the value of our investments.

We can either do asset allocation based on tenure-asset class framework and time our exit from an asset class basis of our cash outflow. Refer to what you read earlier in the chapter – redeem money from a 100% equity-oriented portfolio two years before you need the money and invest the sales proceeds in a fixed income portfolio. The other option is to run a dynamic asset allocation model and guard ourselves against drawdown in the portfolio, when we need the funds.

Let's get back to Simran's portfolio. What if she had invested Rs 10 lakh in ICICI Prudential Multi Asset Fund on 1 January 2008. Table 3.6 shows the value of her portfolio at the end of each year till 2022.

Year	ICICI MAA	Drawdown
31/12/2008	559,486.91	-44.05%
31/12/2009	983,752.00	
31/12/2010	1,192,944.95	
31/12/2011	950,614.64	-20.31%
31/12/2012	1,251,523.25	
31/12/2013	1,446,606.09	
31/12/2014	1,983,324.43	
31/12/2015	1,961,517.90	-1.10%
31/12/2016	2,194,869.05	
31/12/2017	2,805,344.74	
31/12/2018	2,755,745.59	-1.77%
31/12/2019	2,970,283.27	
31/12/2020	3,270,657.40	
31/12/2021	4,389,845.00	
31/12/2022	5,129,235.70	
CAGR	**11.52%**	

Source: Calculation done by the author.

Simran's portfolio would have delivered an 11.52% compounded return and it would have seen lower drawdowns than a 100% equity-oriented portfolio.

Gold is another asset class that has historically outperformed fixed income. Now let us see how a portfolio with only gold as underlying asset has performed during this period. What if Simran had invested Rs 10 lakh in a gold mutual fund on 1 January 2008. Table 3.8 shows the value of her portfolio at the end of each year till 2022.

Table 3.7: Year-End Market Value and Drawdowns of a Gold ETF. Amount Invested Rs 10 Lakh on 1 January 2008

Year	ICICI MAA	Drawdown
2008	1,248,188.11	
2009	1,564,512.61	
2010	1,905,914.56	
2011	2,471,601.94	
2012	2,759,135.22	
2013	2,369,899.48	-14.11%
2014	2,324,519.44	-1.91%
2015	2,151,809.99	-7.43%
2016	2,366,962.57	
2017	2,472,265.12	
2018	2,669,417.26	
2019	3,277,879.36	
2020	4,293,672.37	
2021	3,922,200.22	
2022	4,448,002.43	
CAGR	**10.46%**	

Table 3.8: Year-End Values and Drawdowns of Portfolios. Amount Invested Rs 10 Lakh on 1 January 2008

Year	Fixed Allocation		ICICI MAA		Gold		BSE 500	
	Market Value	Drawdown	Market Value	Drawdown	Market Value	Draw-down	Market Value	Drawdown
31/12/2008	694,247.62	-30.58%	559,486.91	-44.05%	1,248,188.11		415,310.43	-58.47%
31/12/2009	965,029.30		983,752.00		1,564,512.61		790,040.68	
31/12/2010	1,086,519.96		1,192,944.95		1,905,914.56		919,224.12	
31/12/2011	946,795.81	-12.86%	950,614.64	-20.31%	2,471,601.94		667,235.52	-27.41%
31/12/2012	1,136,455.42		1,251,523.25		2,759,135.22		875,406.29	
31/12/2013	1,209,602.00		1,446,606.09		2,369,899.48	-14.11%	903,899.60	
31/12/2014	1,492,239.86		1,983,324.43		2,324,519.44	-1.91%	1,237,972.30	
31/12/2015	1,499,520.98		1,961,517.90	-1.10%	2,151,809.99	-7.43%	1,227,880.65	-0.82%
31/12/2016	1,590,091.04		2,194,869.05		2,366,962.57		1,274,323.00	
31/12/2017	1,885,979.75		2,805,344.74		2,472,265.12		1,732,290.84	
31/12/2018	1,980,802.02		2,755,745.59	-1.77%	2,669,417.26		1,678,906.73	-3.08%
31/12/2019	2,406,273.50		2,970,283.27		3,277,879.36		1,809,041.61	
31/12/2020	2,903,387.03		3,270,657.40		4,293,672.37		2,113,021.80	
31/12/2021	3,003,237.44		4,389,845.00		3,922,200.22		2,749,338.10	
31/12/2022	3,027,549.77		5,129,235.70		4,448,002.43		2,841,107.40	
15 Yrs CAGR	7.66%		11.52%		10.46%		7.21%	

Simran's portfolio would have delivered an 11.52% compounded return and it would have seen lower drawdowns than a 100% equity-oriented portfolio.

There are years when annual returns are lower than 15 years CAGR. The lesson for investors here is that asset classes have cycles. There will be periods when they deliver below long-term average returns and there will be periods when they will deliver above average returns. The unpredictability of these returns and the unforeseeable duration of the cycles is the risk investors need to manage.

Both the methods discussed could have helped investors manage the volatility of the last 20 years. Table 3.8 summarises the portfolios Simran could have invested in on 1 January 2008. Fixed asset allocation, dynamic allocation and a single asset portfolio: gold and equity. I have taken investment in BSE 500 as a single asset equity portfolio. It also captures the drawdowns of these portfolios.

The takeaway is that irrespective of the investor's time horizon a portfolio where the discipline of asset allocation is maintained will outperform a portfolio that is agnostic to rebalancing.

Yes, dear reader, I know you are wondering what if Simran did not have the funds when there were drawdowns in the portfolio. As investors we don't know when we will see drawdowns in our portfolio. How do we consider the cost of cash lying in the bank as it awaits the drawdown? What about taxes? What is the cost of this rebalancing?

It is these variables that make investing difficult. When the stock markets correct by 30%, it takes conviction and experience to allocate additional funds to the equity portfolio. Large corrections in stock markets are caused by turmoil and distress in the economy and the world at large. It was always easy to look back and say I wish I had invested when the stock market was down. After all, hindsight is 20-20.

In October 2008 when stock markets across the world were at a historic low, there was consensus that the models that had run the world's financial markets were broken. That the capitalism and free movement of capital, as we had witnessed in the preceding seven to eight years, would not revive. Nobody saw the upcoming decade of unprecedented rise of stock markets all over the world. It needed an enormous leap of faith to add to one's equity portfolio in October 2008.

In March 2020, as Covid spread and stock markets across the world crashed, 'the world as we knew it was about to come to an end'. We were not sure how and when we would get back to work? When will the next aeroplane take off and when will we go to a cinema hall or have large congregations?

It was difficult to believe in March 2020 that we were about to witness a bull run with stock markets hitting their all-time high before the end of 2021. Stock markets go in a tail-spin because 'the world is coming to an end'.

To liquidate a bank deposit and put the money in an equity mutual fund when 'the world is coming to end' needs gumption that most of us lack. The lack of temperament is just one aspect, discipline is the other. Discipline of keeping money in low interest earning bank deposits and maintaining your fixed income allocation. When the stock market has delivered 37% return in one year, the temptation to break the bank fixed deposit and invest it in a small cap fund that has delivered 58% return in the last one year is difficult to resist.

Investing is as much about emotions, greed and fear, as it is about identifying and investing in the right asset classes. Portfolios underperform and investors fail in achieving their financial goals because they lack the discipline. They can make their lives easier and invest in multi asset allocation mutual fund schemes. This will relieve them of the hassle and the cost of rebalancing the portfolio. This would entail indifference to daily movements of stock markets.

A multi asset allocation fund by design will underperform a pure equity portfolio when the stock market is in a bull run. In a bull run if your friend's small cap portfolio would have gone up by 42% in a year, the value of your multi asset allocation fund may go up by 22%. To retain indifference to sharp increase in stock markets needs discipline and faith in the process. This is where an experienced adviser can help you. We will talk about the need and role of an experienced adviser in one of the chapters.

It is the discipline and the temperament to enforce that discipline that differentiates those who meet their financial goals from those who fail. The converse is also true. There are time periods when equity markets do not deliver any returns. Markets move within a range and investors 'feel nothing is happening'. They think they might as well have invested in commercial real estate, bought gold or bought farm land. It is easy to lose patience and reduce equity allocation when 'nothing seems to be happening'. Investors who can retain equanimity and discipline tend to see their portfolios deliver on their financial goals.

Summary: Diversifying – Investing across different financial assets may not be enough to achieve financial goals. Every financial asset is volatile and its value has drawdowns. Drawdown is the value of an investment decreasing. If the value of the investment sees a drawdown when it is needed to meet financial goals and is less than the expected value, the investment has not fulfilled its purpose. It is important for investors to balance returns and drawdowns if their financial goals are to be achieved. Discipline of asset allocation helps investors achieve balance between returns and drawdowns.

Note: The returns generated by the ICICI Prudential Multi Asset Allocation Fund have been calculated on the basis of public information. The data for these calculations has not been sourced from the ICICI Prudential Asset Management company. It is for illustrative purposes only and should not be considered investment advice. Readers are advised to do their own due diligence.

4

Compounding
God's Gift to Investing

The idea of compounding is so ingrained in our lives that we are indifferent to it. If you have been a regular reader of content written in English for the last ten years, you are reading these words at a speed that's faster than your reading speed from a decade ago. The reason you do not realise that your reading speed has increased manifold is because the increase, if measured weekly, is incremental, but over the years it has compounded. If you read 100 words in a minute 10 years ago, chances are you now read 400 words in a minute. We are so engrossed in the rigour and monotony of daily routine that we ignore the disproportionate rewards of compounding that accrue to our lives.

Think of the one aspect of your life that gives you satisfaction. It could be your work, a sport you enjoy, cooking, playing that musical instrument, anything. Anything that you have been doing on a regular basis for a decade. You are now far more accomplished than you were a decade ago. But if I were to ask you, tell me the ten days in the last ten years when you felt you were better at the task you will struggle to identify those ten days. Chances are you would have felt a marked difference in your proficiency four or five times in the last decade.

Malcolm Gladwell, in his book *Outliers*, writes about ten thousand hours. He writes what differentiates high achievers, in any field, from others is the hours high achievers have put in. He comes up with a figure of ten thousand hours. The ten thousand hours that Gladwell anoints is the time it takes for compounding to do its magic. The difference between 9800 and 10000 hours is 2%, but it is that extra 2% where the magic of compounding plays out.

Table 4.1 illustrates the value of a portfolio growing at 12% annual rate of compounding over a 30-year period.

Table 4.1: End of Period Value of Rs 10,000 Compounding at 12% Every Year

Time Period	Value of Rs 10,000.00
5 Yrs	17,623.00
10 Yrs	31,058.00
15 Yrs	54,735.00
20 Yrs	96,462.00
25 Yrs	170,000.00
30 Yrs	299,599.00

Source: Author's own calculations.

Yes, a compounded annual return of 12% grows the principal by 30 times in 30 years. We have all experienced the benefits of compounding in an asset class we are familiar with – residential real estate. The house your grandfather bought in 1975 for Rs 5 lakh is worth Rs 35.01 cr at the end of 2024. This means the value of that house has gone up by a whopping 700 times. It's an investment that has compounded at 14% over a 50-year period.

You are wondering how an investment can grow 700 times and still deliver only a 14% annual return. Well, that's 14% compounded over a 50-year period. Table 4.2 captures the value of the house at the end of every year assuming it was bought on 1 January 1975.

Table 4.2: Year-End Value of a House Bought on 1 January 1975

Year	End of Year Value
1975	570,000.00
1976	649,800.00
1977	740,772.00
1978	844,480.08
1979	962,707.29
1980	1,097,486.31
1981	1,251,134.40
1982	1,426,293.21
1983	1,625,974.26
1984	1,853,610.66
1985	2,113,116.15
1986	2,408,952.41
1987	2,746,205.75
1988	3,130,674.55
1989	3,568,968.99
1990	4,068,624.65
1991	4,638,232.10
1992	5,287,584.59
1993	6,027,846.44
1994	6,871,744.94
1995	7,833,789.23
1996	8,930,519.72
1997	10,180,792.48
1998	11,606,103.43
1999	13,230,957.91

Year	End of Year Value
2000	15,083,292.01
2001	17,194,952.89
2002	19,602,246.30
2003	22,346,560.78
2004	25,475,079.29
2005	29,041,590.39
2006	33,107,413.05
2007	37,742,450.87
2008	43,026,394.00
2009	49,050,089.16
2010	55,917,101.64
2011	63,745,495.87
2012	72,669,865.29
2013	82,843,646.43
2014	94,441,756.93
2015	107,663,602.90
2016	122,736,507.30
2017	139,919,618.33
2018	159,508,364.89
2019	181,839,535.98
2020	207,297,071.02
2021	236,318,660.96
2022	269,403,273.49
2023	307,119,731.78
2024	350,116,494.23

Source: Author's calculations for illustrative purpose only.

See the value of the house at the end of 1984. That is the time when your father did not think of the house as a great investment and instead of chipping in to buy the adjacent plot with your grandfather and uncle, he decided to spend the money on the newly launched Maruti 800.

By the end of 1994, the house was now valuable enough for your grandfather to start thinking how to give it away to his children, all of whom by now have realised how valuable the house is. By the end of 2004, if the granddad has still not figured out what to do with the house, chances are it's not helping your father's relationship with his siblings.

By the end of 2014, if the house is still in the name of your grandfather, your father and his siblings are just about managing to stay on talking terms. In 2025 if the house is still in your grandfather's name, you, your father and your sibling have had a couple of conversations with your lawyer friend to understand the intricacies of succession laws in India.

That is what compounding does to the portfolio, provided as an investor you have the patience and the 'balance sheet strength' to stay the course. What do I mean by balance sheet strength? The ability to retain the investment in case of an unforeseen expenses that cannot be met with your regular income.

Assume in the year 1987, your grandfather had sold off the house to meet expenses – a major loss in the business, or unexpected expense on medical treatment of your grand-mom. Or perhaps he'd sold off the house and given away the proceeds to your father and his siblings.

You would now be telling stories of your granddad's house and how much it would have been worth today if only he had not sold it in 1987. The key to compounding is the discipline of asset allocation.

One of the primary reasons why growth assets – assets that give real returns – get liquidated is an unexpected or an unplanned expense.

We have seen the power of compounding, but the key to a portfolio benefitting from compounding is the ability of investors to stay invested. This ability is vastly enhanced if the investors maintain liquidity for unforeseen events or contingencies. This is where I would like to introduce you to the idea of liquidity premium/discount and illiquidity premium/discount.

A premium is the return that an investor gets over and above the risk-free return from an investment. Discount is the return that the investor gets that is below the risk-free return. Let us try and understand this concept with an example.

A bank deposit with a bank in India is one of the safest investments. Let us see the difference in the rate of interest that State Bank of India offers to its savings account holders and the returns it offers to its fixed deposits holders. The return in the former is 3% where the rate of interest in a one-year duration fixed deposit is 7%. Why is there a difference?

Money in the savings bank account kept for a year is as safe as money in a year-long fixed deposit. Why then, do the fixed deposit holders get a higher rate of interest? The reason is the illiquidity premium and the liquidity discount. Money from the savings bank account can be withdrawn at any point of time.

Depositors can walk into an ATM and withdraw anytime, do an online money transfer or use UPI. They don't have to give instructions to the bank to get access to their funds. The funds are always available, depositors have liquidity.

The fixed deposit on the other hand is a contract where the depositor has made a commitment. A commitment that she will not withdraw the money before the end of one year. The money will stay invested in the bank for a period of one year. She is forgoing access to her funds and giving up liquidity.

The return she gets over and above her savings bank account interest rate is the illiquidity premium.

She gets 3% on her savings account because she has liquidity and she gets 7% on her fixed deposit because she forgoes liquidity. The 4% that she gets over and above the savings account interest rate is the illiquidity premium.

When we assess and build our expectation of return from an asset class, we need to consider the illiquidity premium the investment generates and the liquidity discount that will accrue to the investor.

The reason growth asset classes, equities and real estate, deliver higher real returns is because investors forego liquidity. You cannot wake up in the morning and sell your house by noon; technically you can, but then it will be a distress sale and you will most probably get a return lower than the market value.

This applies to equities too. Yes, you can at the click of a button liquidate your equity holdings but doing that could lead to sub-par returns.

It is this seeming presence of liquidity, an equity holding in a publicly traded company that can be liquidated easily, that makes it easy for investors to miss the illiquidity premium that is built in the asset class. If the investors display the discipline of staying invested and do not liquidate the investment at the first signs of turmoil in the market, they end up with optimal returns. Benefits of compounding accrue and lead to the value of investments growing multifold if the investors identify the illiquidity premium built in the asset class. The reason your grandfather's house is worth what it is today is because it has compounded at a rate that includes the illiquidity premium.

As an investor you do demand an illiquidity premium, you will never book a fixed deposit at a rate of interest that is similar to a savings rate of interest. *Usi bhaw pe paisa kyon lock karun* (why should I lock in the money at the same interest rate). You should assess investments in your portfolio on the same principle.

Why should I invest in a life insurance policy that locks my money for 5/10/15 years if it does not give me a return that justifies illiquidity? If my financial adviser tells me the money can be withdrawn at any time and that there is no lock-in period for my investment, what am I missing out on?

We have discussed illiquidity premium and its converse liquidity discount. Let us now talk about liquidity premium and illiquidity discount. Yes, there are asset classes and investment instruments that give investors an additional return because they can be liquidated at anytime and anywhere in the world. Gold is an example of an investment that can be liquidated anytime and anywhere in the world.

This is because it is a universally accepted medium of exchange. We discussed earlier in the book how you can use gold to trade with anyone anywhere in the world. It is this intrinsic feature that makes gold a valuable asset. Buying gold is not an investment in an economic activity.

When investors buy shares in a company, they are investing in a business that is involved in an economic activity – making and selling of goods or services. When an investor invests in a bond, she knows the borrower is capable of paying interest and repaying the principal because they have an underlying source of revenue generated by their business. In case of investing in a government bond, they know the government can repay by levying taxes.

An investment in gold delivers returns because it is a universally accepted medium of exchange and can be liquidated and converted to cash or goods at any time anywhere in the world. The liquid nature of the asset earns the investors the return that gold as an asset class delivers. The other asset that delivers a return because it is universally accepted and can be liquidated anywhere and anytime is US dollar. The US dollar, like any currency issued by a central bank of a sovereign state, is a promise made to the bearer that the US government will honour the commitment made to the tune of the denomination of the currency note. The promise is accepted across the world and a part of the reason why the holders of US dollars make returns on it vis-a-vis other currencies is that there are buyers of the currency available anywhere and anytime in the world.

Let us now close the discussion by covering the illiquidity discount. We discussed how a savings account gives a lower rate of interest than a fixed deposit because it is liquid. Investors have to pay an illiquidity discount when they sell their investments in distress. An example of distress sale is the sale of property. Real estate as an asset class is not traded on the exchange like equities. The price discovery of the asset is a negotiation between the buyer and the seller. A sale done under the pressure of a timeline leads to the buyer getting a discount on prevailing market price of the property. A transaction like this leads to the investors accruing an illiquidity discount.

As we assess various investment options and returns that various investments will deliver, it is important that we understand the extent of illiquidity premium/discount in these investments. This is critical if we want our investment to benefit from the power of compounding. If an investment can be liquidated at any time, it does not mean that it does not carry an illiquidity premium and just because an asset cannot be liquidated at short notice does not mean that it does not have illiquidity discount.

The next time you invest, ask how long will be the tenure of the investment? Will the returns from the investment compensate for the time duration? If an investment is offering liquidity are there any costs associated with that liquidity? Costs could be penalties for early withdrawals or sub-par returns.

As investors one of the reasons that we miss out on compounding is that we misunderstand the relationship between the seemingly liquid nature of the investment and the return trade-off that comes with it. It is always better to assess before you invest rather than miss out on the magic of compounding.

Summary: Compounding is God's gift to humanity. We all are aware of and beneficiaries of compounding in our daily lives. Think of the speed with which you are reading this sentence now; compare it with your reading speed a decade ago. Every investment benefits from the power of compounding. The key to getting the power of compounding work for you is not to sell in your investment is distress or in panic. You can avoid distress sale when you have the balance sheet strength. Balance sheet strength is your ability to meet unexpected expenses without selling your investment. Assess the cost of selling an investment and losing out on the benefits of compounding before you invest.

5

Prepare for a Rainy Day

Life is a risk management exercise. We wake up and blink our eyes; we do not want to stumble as we get used to the daylight. We start our day by managing the risk of injury. We walk and cook with care. We take care of our health because our body is prone to sickness. We have risk management tools for every risk we face. The tools include mental models of the costs we pay and are willing to pay for managing risks. We assign probabilities to unfortunate events that may call upon us and prepare for them.

We prepare via trade-offs. Do I save for retirement or should I take that vacation? Another helping of the dessert or satisfaction of what the weighing machine will read. Do I drive fast and save time, enjoy the exhilaration or do I enjoy the sights and sounds? We assign the risk and return trade-offs and if you are reading this, it means you are alive and your risk management works. This is a simple conclusion.

We are alive does not mean that we haven't had accidents. It just means we haven't had a fatal accident.

We have had our share of physical accidents – broken bones and stitches. Emotional accidents – divorces and estranged family members. Financial accidents – money invested in a plot of land that refuses to appreciate, loans that are difficult to service.

We have managed because luck has also played its part. We know of people who weren't so lucky and are in stress. The way our risk management process works is intuitive and a function of our lived experience. We either learn from our own experiences or we learn from other people's experiences. We understand the cause and effect but are confident of managing the downside via natural instinct.

I 'know' how fast I can drive.

I 'know' how much alcohol I can have and still drive.

I 'know' I am healthy and I don't really need that extra health insurance cover.

I 'know' I will get my salary at the end of the month so why not swipe that credit card on an impulse purchase.

Some of us keep an account of our expenses and maintain spreadsheets that capture our income and expenses and try to manage financial risk. It's a great habit, more power to those who do that.

Most of us do not have this discipline and carry the same indiscipline to other aspects of our life. We don't maintain a record of how much sugar we consume on a daily basis and what impact that consumption has on our health. We do not keep a record of our physical activity, our exercise routine to tally it with our fitness goals. We do not keep a track of how much time we spend on our mobile devices and what impact it has on our cognitive ability and our attention span. We tell ourselves we know what we are doing and this is the best we can do. That we are managing the risks and are doing a good job of it. Till the penny drops and the risk plays out.

Something untoward may happen suddenly – for example, you get a bonus that is less than what your boss made you believe you would get; or a car accident; or you get to know of a colleague who died of a sudden heart attack; or you realise you can't read a five-

thousand-word essay in one go. Anything untoward can happen. When we think, we realise how lucky we have been that the loss of income, or accident, or a critical illness has not stuck us.

However, when something untoward happens, what follows is, likely, a response that is no different from what we did earlier. We rationalise saying, 'this was just bad luck, I have been driving like this for years and nothing has ever happened before' and we continue to live the way we do. Another probable response is that we panic and try to find a way out post facto. I should reduce my weight by ten kilos in ten weeks. Let me find a health insurance policy that will cover my pre-existing illnesses; I will pay whatever is the premium. I will convert my credit card outstanding into a 'no interest' EMI and pay it over 24 months. An unstructured risk management framework is how most of us live.

Yes, some of us live a disciplined, structured life where we have pre-empted and planned for these risks, but most of us have not. Then there are risks that cannot be anticipated. The unknown unknowns. *Kisi ne socha he nahin tha ye bhi ho sakta hai* (no one ever thought something like this might happen).

Data on the number of families that have slipped to a lower income group post a prolonged illness of family members, or the earning member of the family losing her job is hard to get in India. We don't have personal bankruptcy laws in India, and no support and guidance on how to deal with personal bankruptcies. However, we all know of individuals who have seen drastic changes in their lives because of unforeseen events. What can we do? It's not that we are unaware of the risks that we face; after all we manage them to the best of our ability. We are all constrained by the limits of our bounded rationality.

What is Bounded Rationality? Bounded rationality means our decision making is a function of the access to information and our ability to process that information at the time of decision making. Let us try and understand this with an example.

You need to get yourself a dress for a friend's birthday party. You go to a nearby mall and drop in at the stores of all the brands you like to wear and see if something catches your fancy. While you are at the mall you also check out dresses on Myntra, Amazon or any of the apps that you use online. You finally choose a dress, pay for it, dress up and reach the party happy with the choice you made. As you step in you see that a friend at the party is wearing the same dress and lo and behold, she got it at a 20% discount last week! You are disappointed and blame yourself for not keeping a lookout for such deals.

You make your peace by acknowledging the scope of your bounded rationality. You tell yourself you were not looking to buy a dress last week. That you had other things in your life going on for you to go window shopping or surf online and check out the dresses. When you decided you needed a new dress and found the time to shop, you could only access as many stores as you could and access as many apps as you did. Your decision of buying the dress was influenced by the information you had when you went shopping and your ability at that time to process all the information. You try not to think too much about the discount your friend got and enjoy the party. This is how we live our lives and manage risk.

Let us try and understand how bounded rationality influences our risk management with another example. Your health is of utmost importance to you. You decide the quality of your drinking water is something you will not compromise on. You find the best water purifier and install it. You do not compromise. You need the best water purifier for your family and are willing to spend a meaningful sum of money on a water purifier, you get it serviced regularly and the salesman that sold you the purifier convinced you to buy an annual service contract. You have paid for that annual service contract too. All this does not guarantee that you or anyone in your family will never suffer from a water-borne disease. It's you managing the risk of water-borne disease to the best of your bounded rationality.

We are limited by how much information we have when we are making decisions and constrained by our ability to process that information. With our lived experience and with access to technology, we expand the limits of our bounded rationality every day. Is there a way in which we can expand the scope of our bounded rationality without having to live through an experience. A way that will help us manage our life risks better.

Yes, there is! Let us call this framework – Probability-Impact Matrix.

Figure 5.1: Probability-Impact Matrix

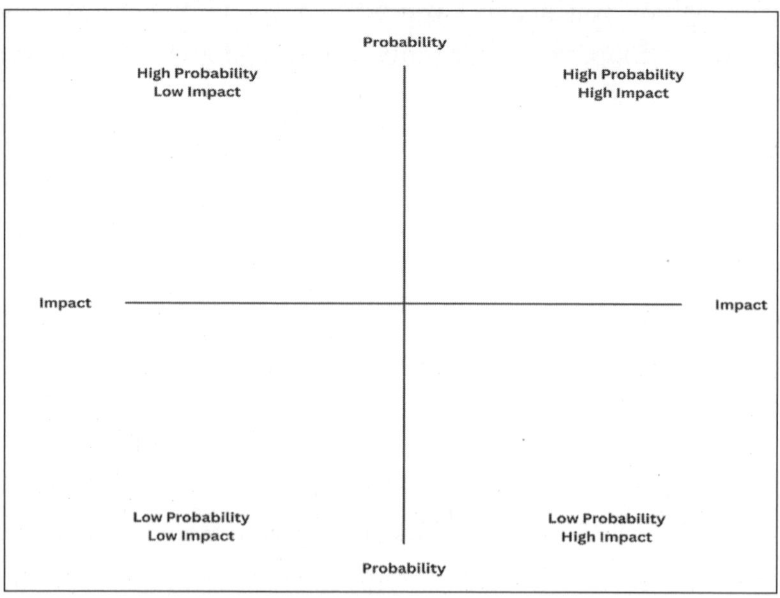

Source: Framework by Jalaj Varshney.

There are events that have low probability of happening but will have a disproportionate impact on your life and then there are events that have high probability of happening but will have a low impact on your life. These are just the two extremes of this matrix. Every event in life is a combination of these two.

An example of a 'low probability high impact' event is the single bread-earner of the family dying in an aeroplane crash, and an example of a 'high probability low impact' event is you suffering from a common cold and having to take a sick leave. You can corroborate from your lived experience that a high probability low impact event is something your existing risk management framework has handled well. Most of these events cause minor inconveniences and we move on.

It is the 'low probability high impact' events that are the real test of our risk management. While we understand and can enumerate a list of low probability high impact events, losing our job, a critical illness, a natural calamity that wipes out our physical assets or an 'unexpected' stock market crash that reduces the value of the portfolio by 50%.

What we cannot do is to time these risks playing out. Nobody in January 2020 foresaw the Covid lockdowns. Not only can we not time the occurrences of these risks, but there are also unknown unknowns − risks that we cannot imagine and risks that we have no experience of managing. Not only can we not predict the timing of life disrupting events, but we also don't even know the nature of risks that surround us. If in December 2019 I had told you the world will lock itself down in March 2020 because an experiment has gone wrong in a laboratory, chances are you would have laughed at me and never taken me seriously after that.

How does one prepare for these black swan events? It is not if, but when you will face a black swan event in your life. A black swan event can be personal. It is a black swan event in your life when the rest of the world carries on and you are the only one impacted by it. A rare cancer is an unfortunate and a black swan event in the patient's life. How does one deal with a black swan event? The way the modern world works, cash in your bank account is indispensable.

If you have cash or liquid assets in your portfolio, you have given yourself a chance of surviving a low probability high impact event. An income interruption aggravates the intensity of the high impact event. If you lose your job and do not have liquid assets to tide you over for the time it will take to find another job, you will end up liquidating your investments and miss out on real returns. The other option is to borrow; there is a chance you will not get a loan and even if you do it will be at a high interest rate, and you may fall in a

debt trap. The way to minimize the impact of life-changing events in our life is to classify all the risks that you can foresee in a 2 by 2 matrix. All risks in your life will fall in this matrix. 'Low probability High Impact' and 'High Probability Low Impact'.

Let's make a list of the risks we encounter in our lives and see where they fall in the matrix. Go on, pick a pencil and write down where these risks fit in your risk management matrix.

a) You lose your job.

b) You get inflicted by a critical illness.

c) You meet with a minor accident.

d) The bank where you keep all your money goes bankrupt.

e) You get stuck in a traffic jam and miss the train/flight for an important event.

f) You are stuck in a traffic jam and reach half an hour late for a critical business meeting.

g) Your phone gets stolen at the food court.

h) Your pocket gets picked at the mall.

i) You slip in the bathroom and break your bones.

j) One of your parents is hospitalised and they need immediate monetary help.

This is not an exhaustive list of events that can happen in your life that may cause physical, emotional or financial stress. You can write down more events and fit them into this matrix.

The next step is to assess how many of these risks you will be able to manage better if you had liquid cash in your portfolio. There are risks that cannot be managed by money in a savings bank account. Your bank balance will not help you reach that critical business meeting on time. Money in the bank is useless if the bank goes bankrupt. Here is how I have categorised these ten risks.

Please note we have our own unique way of categorising these risks. We are unique and how we categorise these risks is a function of our lived experiences. Let us now ask which of these risks I can handle, without selling investments that are compounding at real return, if I maintain liquidity in the portfolio.

An income interruption, caused by a job loss, can only be managed if there is money in the bank. You can liquidate your assets in an eventuality like this but then you miss out on benefits

Figure 5.2: Events Categorised on a Probability-Impact Matrix

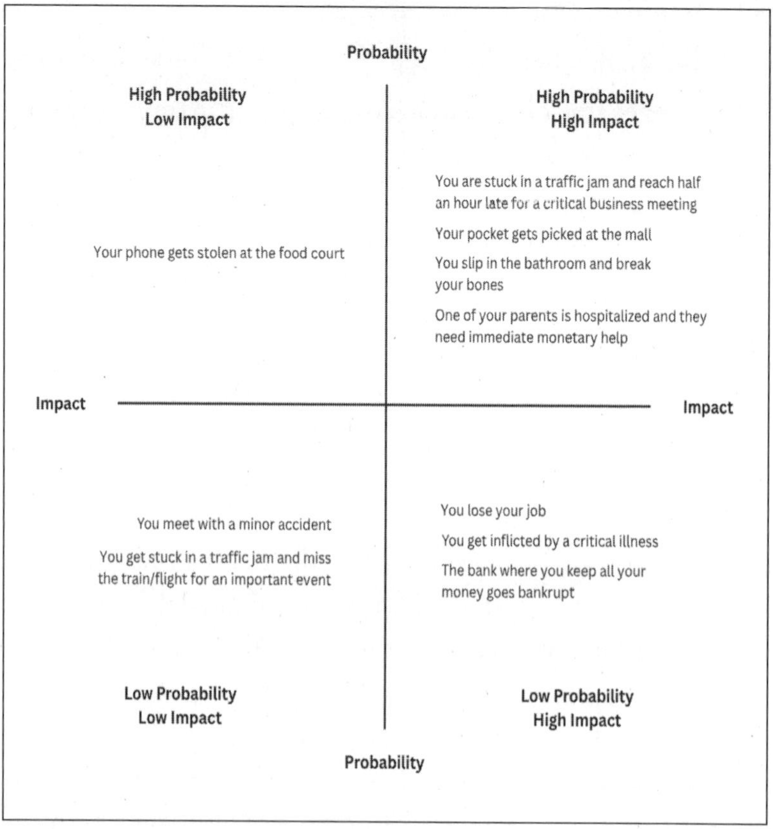

Source: Framework by Jalaj Varshney.

of compounding, your portfolio will underperform and you will miss out on your financial goals.

The other aspect of liquidating your growth assets when you lose your job is that you will end up liquidating in distress and may get an amount that is lower than the fair value of the asset. There is a good chance that when you lose your job, there is turmoil in the broader economy and the stock markets are going through a downturn. This means that the equity component of your investments is below its peak market value. If you liquidate now, you have redeemed your investments in times of drawdowns.

If you try and liquidate a part of your real estate investment to tide over till you get another job, it will be distress sale at lower than fair value, as the urgency of sale will be used by the buyer to bring down the price. You suffer a double whammy; not only do you miss out on compounding that accrues to your investment, you also end up liquidating your assets at a price lower than what they would have got you if it were not a distress sale. There are risks that can be managed better if we have cash in the bank.

Yes, cash in a bank account is a depreciating asset. Savings bank interest is less than the rate of inflation, which means cash delivers a negative real return. *Savings bank mein paise rakhna is waste of money, isse accha to kahin invest kar do.* (Keeping money in savings bank account is a waste of money; it is better to invest that money somewhere.) Yes, we have all heard this statement and I believe in it too. However, to consider money in a savings account only as a poor investment is to ignore its other vital role. Money in the bank account is an insurance product.

Think of the low return that the savings bank account gives you as a cost. A cost you bear, just like you bear the cost of premium payments for health or motor insurance policies that you buy. You renew your health insurance policy every year, irrespective of any claims you may or may not have made. Insurance premium is a cost and you are happy to bear it.

Start to think of money in your savings account as an insurance premium. It is an insurance that will help you manage the risk of low probability high impact events in your life. This brings us to the question, how much money one should keep in a savings account as an insurance against high impact risks. There is no one answer to this question.

These questions will help to get the answer to these questions.

a) How long will the income interruption last? How long will it take you to get another job?

b) The answer to this question should be in months. Will I get a job in 3 or 6 or 12 months?

c) While I look for another job, do I want to sustain my existing lifestyle or will I reduce my expenses?

The answer to these questions will help you arrive at the minimum sum of money you will need to save for every month that you miss out on your regular income. A common risk that leads to financial stress and households slipping down in their economic status is critical illness. Medical expenses can bankrupt individuals and families. The coverage of health insurance in India is a good indicator of how we underestimate the benefits of buying a health insurance product. If you are planning for an expense that cannot be met with your existing income, say, a critical illness to a family member, then in the absence of health insurance, cash in the bank account is what you need. An unexpected event, in the absence of liquid assets, leads to liquidation of growth assets, or sale of assets meant for the next generation like gold or family jewellery or borrowing.

Loans taken to tide over unexpected expenses put enormous pressure on personal finances and can lead to the most well-constructed financial plans go awry. We all know from anecdotal instances of individuals and families going bankrupt as they try to meet unplanned expenses. This brings us to the question as to how much money one should keep aside to meet an unforeseen medical expense.

After all, any allocation to a contingency fund, kept in low-yielding liquid investments, reduces allocation to growth assets and probability of the portfolio delivering on long-term financial goals. There is a trade-off for how much of your future earnings are you willing to sacrifice for managing a low probability high impact event. Insurance is what we need to manage this risk. Maintaining a savings bank account balance is an insurance as is a health insurance policy. The best way to manage an exorbitant medical expense is to buy health insurance. Buy it young and buy a large cover.

Yes, the premium will have to be paid; yes, there is a good chance you will not claim with the insurance company for years and still pay the premiums. Yes, the premium payment means that you can't afford that weekend getaway, you are unable to allocate more money to an equity mutual fund and there is less money to buy clothes or the new iPhone.

The idea of saving for a rainy day, by definition means compromise on your lifestyle. It is a sacrifice. On top of buying a large health insurance cover, I suggest, you keep cash in a bank account and not spend it on a three-day trip to Sri Lanka with friends and family. Yes, I am a killjoy.

Before you ignore what you just read and say it loud in your head – One life to live, why be so scared. Play this scenario in your mind – your child or mother is in the hospital and the doctors say they will not start the treatment till you make a deposit of 25% of the expected bill. You do not have ample medical insurance; your portfolio is in investments that cannot be liquidated or is meant for your child's admission in a college she has worked hard for years. The only other options are to borrow or sell the gold ring your mother gifted your spouse when you got married. The bank will take three to five days to give you a loan or you ask friends and family to lend you a hand.

Think of how you will feel when you make that phone call. How does that feel compared to possession of the latest smartphone or photographs of that vacation in Thailand? This is a very subjective question and we will all have our own answers. I have still not helped you come up with the answer to the question: How much money do you keep in your savings account for a contingency like this?

Life is about making trade-offs. How much are we willing to sacrifice today for a better future or how much are we willing to save today to meet an expense that you have no clue as to when it will be incurred and what it will cost. This chapter is to make you think about this trade-off.

Life is what it is, there will come a moment when a low probability high impact event will play out.

Any preparation for that day is better than no preparation at all.

Summary: Everything we do in life is aimed at managing risks. The act of walking and cooking carefully is a risk-management exercise. List down what you did today and you will realise how much you did today was to manage the risk of your standard of living going down. We manage these risks to the best of our ability. This ability can go up substantially if we prepare for events that have low probability of occurring but can have a disproportionate impact on our lifestyle. Our ability to manage these low-probability, high-impact events determine the returns on our investments. We have to formulate ways and means that will help us manage the risk of low probability-high impact events and stick to them at all costs.

6

Get a Financial Adviser
A Good One

At the end of 2013, Roger Federer, one of the greatest tennis players of all times, got former world number one men's tennis player Stefan Edberg to work as his coach. This was after Federer had won 17 grand slams, held the world number 1 tennis ranking for 237 weeks and had cemented his place as a legend of the game.

Why did Federer get a coach? Why do professionals, across occupations and vocations, seek advice and oftentimes reach out to experts from other fields to improve their performance? We all live our professional lives in what I call an activity trap. We do the same tasks every day for weeks, months and years and end up with a routine. This helps us become efficient but we lose our ability to see how we can eke out marginal gains from our efforts or become more productive. This is where an external reviewer helps. They help us see a new point of view; identify areas of marginal improvements; help us get better.

In India we live in an age of over communication. We have five broadsheet business newspapers, the United States of America has one. We have multiple business channels on TV in English and in Indian languages. Business and capital markets news in the USA is dominated by one news channel. Then there is the infinite universe of 'fin influencers' that flood us with information via social media.

The competitive landscape of business news has led to dumbing down of a serious topic.

The clickbait nature of content has led to a vicious cycle. Investors fall for investment advice that does not serve their purpose. When the returns don't accrue for the advice is generic and there is no downside for the adviser, they sell their equity portfolio and revert to low-yield assets like fixed income or illiquid assets like real estate and traditional insurance plans. The flip side of this is that when investors see high returns in their equity portfolio in their early trades, they get lulled into a false sense of confidence, go overboard and when the cycle turns, they lose their shirt.

A portfolio that meets investor goals needs time. The time and effort it takes is akin to a marathon. It is not a sprint. We do not build stamina and the endurance for a marathon when coached by multiple sprinters with dubious track records of running any meaningful distance on a regular basis. The key to a portfolio that helps you achieve your financial goals is to have the right adviser by your side.

Yes, you can access all the accumulated human wisdom for free, just google the words how to grow your money and you will end up with enough pages to last a lifetime. You can see videos of world's finest investors and finance professionals talk about their investment process for free on YouTube.

Why not do it yourself? Why bother finding an adviser? It's not like a portfolio adviser will guarantee you that your financial goals will be met. How does an adviser help!

Let's step back. If you have a portfolio of financial assets there is a very good chance that you already have a financial adviser and have had bitter experiences with multiple financial advisers. In India, a Life Insurance Corporation of India (LIC) agent is often the first financial adviser one meets. If you are a salaried professional, an LIC agent will call the month you started work.

He or she is probably a relative of yours or a family friend. This agent convinced you to save and save early. You were told that the insurance policy will help you retire comfortably and how it will give you income at regular intervals and to top it all, the kind agent also offered to pay half of the first policy premium. You recalled this conversation when HR sent out an e-mail to submit proof of tax saving investments and called up the agent. The agent turned up within the hour. You signed a form that she said she will fill up later, took the cheque and sent you the first premium receipt the very next day. It's been ten years. You pay the annual premium of the policy and you still don't know how much money you will get when the policy matures and there is a good chance you don't even know when the policy will mature.

If you are one of those lucky ones who escaped this adventure then chances are your first ever financial adviser was your bank's relationship manager. The smooth talking, uber confident young banker who conveyed the impression that a unit linked insurance plan (ULIP) is the best thing that can happen to you. How an investment in a ULIP will help you buy that dream car, house in the hills and retire early. That you only need to pay premium for five years and at the end of those five years you will not only have saved taxes but will have enough money to fulfil all your dreams. The sample illustration showed an 8% annual return, but the underlying fund generated 34% return in the last one year and that is the annual return you can expect. Imagine your corpus when the policy matures!

The sales pitch was reinforced by charts and graphs that showed how stock market in India had grown at an impressive rate over the last decade, how it was primed to go up further for years to come and if you do not invest today, you will live to regret. The relationship manager was accompanied by an insurance specialist and for the final nudge perhaps the branch manager had walked in and offered you his warm smile and a cold drink. All to get you to sign the application form. The application you were assured will be filled up by the considerate branch service staff and that you will get a copy of the filled-up form with the policy document.

The adviser sounded like he knew all about the product, was well versed in the working of capital markets, carried an aura of competence and had the backing of the institution he worked for. Numbers were thrown around on how many clients have invested in the insurance product, how many crores of assets were under management, credentials of the fund managers were shared with gusto and between their confidence and your lack of knowledge and experience, the life insurance policy was bought and the first premium paid.

Once the first policy premium is paid, the LIC agent only calls you to remind you that the next premium is due or to press upon you why you should buy another policy. The bank's relationship manager has now either moved to another bank or got a promotion and does not take your phone call if you ask him how the insurance policy he sold you is helping you meet your financial goals. That is how you got initiated to the world of investments and financial advisers. Yes, it didn't get any better after that. Lesson learnt, you refused to engage with anyone trying to sell you a life insurance policy.

As you move up in life the bank now has given you a relationship manager who talks about 'new age' products like Portfolio Management Services (PMS) and Alternative Investment Funds. These are bespoke strategies that will give you fantastic returns. You are told these products are not mass-market products and cater only to high-net-worth individuals. These are customised portfolios, your relationship manager invited you for drinks and dinner with the fund manager at a five-star hotel, where you are given a chance to interact with the fund manager. The fund manager is a smooth, sober gentleman who gives you the lowdown on how India is at the cusp of sustained economic growth that will give you a once-in-a-lifetime investment opportunity. A case is built for investment in a theme that will outperform the broader markets. Slides with graphs and growth projections are accompanied by words like secular trends, judicious capital allocation, low leverage, MOATS and long track record of earnings growth. This time you check what are the fund management charges, how long your money will be locked in and if there is a recurring commitment of investing every year for the product to make you the returns the fund manager and your relationship manager promise.

Two years after you invested, your relationship manager has again moved and the new relationship manager tells you that the fund management strategy has failed. He tells you the bank has had a hard look at the performance of the fund manager and the asset management company and has decided that this specific PMS strategy is no longer part of their recommended set of investments. That you should redeem the investment and consider an investment in another PMS which the bank thinks is the strategy that is bound to deliver returns that will be far more than the returns the current PMS has delivered. You are not sure, but the RM makes a case for redemption. He mentions the low cost of exit and how that cost will be offset by superior returns the new strategy will deliver. You decide to do what the adviser says and two years later, the investment has still not delivered the returns you were promised four years ago and the latest relationship manager is suggesting you exit this investment and reinvest in a ULIP. This is how the financial advisers have treated your hard-earned money and this chapter is on why you should have one. Why am I being daft, you say.

Yes, in a world where all the information is easily accessible, you can manage your money yourself. There are plenty of YouTube videos where those who have been there and done that tell you where to invest for free. There are platforms and apps that let you invest for free and then there are books. Books that tell you how to invest and make millions. Why bother with an adviser then? The only thing an adviser has ever done is move your money from one investment plan to another while he won an insurance contest and got promoted!

I will try and answer this question in two parts. The first is where I will tell you what is wrong with the advisers you worked with and in the second part I will explain how the right adviser can help you achieve your financial goals and justify the cost you will pay.

So what was wrong about the advisers you have had. Let us start with the LIC agent. A life insurance agent is NOT a financial adviser. He or she is what their designation says. A LIC agent is an agent, the agent of the insurance company. He or she is NOT

YOUR adviser. They are agents of the company they represent. There, you see, the conflict of interest is right there. An LIC agent makes money if they are able to sell you the most profitable product for the insurance company. An LIC agent is no different from a salesman at a saree shop, incentivised to sell you the saree with the highest profit margin for the shopkeeper. Add to that the fact that the agent offers you an insurance policy from one company. They may be agents of multiple life insurance companies, but when they come visiting they have already made up their mind on what product they want to sell you. How else are they assuring you that they will take care of your first policy premium! The conflict of interest is a given.

Why did your bank relationship fail you as a good financial adviser? The RM failed because she is not incentivised to make your portfolio deliver on your financial goals. She is incentivised to generate the highest fee income for the bank. An insurance product is the most-high-margin financial product. The next time somebody asks you to buy a life insurance policy, ask them how much commission will they or their bank make on the amount you invest. If they are honest, you will be surprised by the answer.

The incentive or bonus that the relationship manager makes is linked to the commission on sale of insurance products that she generates for the bank. The amount of commission income that she generates has a weightage in her key deliverables. Her monetary benefits and her promotion in the bank are linked to her ability to generate commission income via sale of insurance products.

When you visit your bank's branch next, notice the number of certificates of appreciation for selling life insurance products, the photographs that your relationship manager has on her desk, taken at events and conferences, with the senior management of the bank, for winning an 'Insurance Contest' and ask her if there is an 'insurance contest' going on in the branch.

If you get a chance, walk into the branch manager's cabin. You will see the number of certificates he has accumulated over the years; they are an indicator of his career in the bank. Chances are there's a certificate that says this was the number one branch in insurance sales in the cluster/circle/zone of the bank's branch network in the last quarter. Not only on display are the certificates he has been given for selling insurance as the manager of this branch, he also has retained the certificates and the awards he had won as a personal banker, as a relationship manager, and as the manager of other branches before he landed up as the manager of your branch. The 'star' performer of the branch is the relationship manager/banker who has qualified for the Million Dollar Round Table.

It is the misaligned incentive structure: your relationship manager, who is supposed to be your financial adviser and help you achieve your financial goals, is incentivised on products that generate a higher revenue for the bank instead of products that meet your financial goals. Before the PMS product was advised to you, did the relationship manager check with you what was your risk appetite, what was your overall asset allocation, what was your allocation in equities? Did the relationship manager explain how the PMS would complement your existing investments? Were you informed of the annual expense the fund manager would charge and were you told about the exit loads and the taxes applicable on the capital gains. It is likely that most of these questions were not asked and the relationship manager did not cover these points when she pitched you the product.

When her successor advised you to get out of the strategy and move the money to another PMS, the reason given was the underperformance of the fund or, in case the value of the investment had grown, you were advised to book profits before the market corrects! What you experienced with your PMS investment is called, in the language of the wealth management industry, churning of the portfolio. When the adviser is not able to solicit incremental funds from the client, she redeems a client's existing investment and re-invests the proceeds in another investment product. Why do the advisers, especially the bank relationship managers, do that? The reason is: yes, you guessed it right – misaligned incentives. Your bank's relationship manager is incentivised to get flows in the 'preferred or select or curated' set of investment products. The relationship manager and the bank make more money if you get out of your existing investment and reinvest that money in another investment product.

The churning of the portfolio is disadvantageous to the investor because of two reasons. One is the cost – every time the investor exits an investment, she ends up paying taxes on the profit she made. Exiting an investment before it has achieved its original purpose does not help her meet her financial goals and paying taxes on those gains only to reinvest the post-tax proceeds is a waste of your hard-earned money. The other reason is the cost of missing out on compounding. Recall our discussion on compounding earlier in the book. Every time you redeem an investment you reduce the probability of compounding kicking in. An exit and reinvestment, by definition, means you incur the cost of exit and the ensuing taxes. This implies that your reinvestment amount is less than the value of your investment when you exited it.

Let me explain this with an example. Assume you had invested Rs 50 lakh in a PMS product, the relationship manager advised you to redeem it when the value of the investment was Rs 80 lakh. That is a gain of Rs 30 lakh on which you end paying taxes to the tune of Rs 3.75 lakh. Post taxes, your net investment is 76.25 lakh. You not only ended up paying taxes that were avoidable, you lost benefits of compounding on Rs 3.75 lakh of your hard-earned money. If the portfolio had continued to grow at 15%, that's 15.17 lakh of gains lost over the next ten years.

Build the probability that the product where you have reinvested the money will give returns that are lower than the returns your existing PMS is generating. You end up where you have paid taxes on profits you need not have booked, as your financial goals were yet to be met. You miss out on compounding all of your original investment and you have taken the risk of investing in a product that may not deliver returns similar to or better than your current investment.

You are now aware of the fact that the incentive structure of your insurance agent and your bank's relationship manager is misaligned. It is now safe to ask: isn't that the case with all investment advisers? You are right. The biggest handicap for investors, when they deal with financial advisers, is conflict of interest.

In the case of insurance products, agents make a substantial commission on the day you buy the insurance policy; these commissions can go up to 40% of the first premium that you pay. They also get commissions on the renewal premium that you will pay that can be as low as 1/20th of the first-year premium that you paid. This is one of the reasons why your bank relationship manager is always on the lookout for 'reviewing' all your existing insurance policies and suggesting that you surrender a policy that is not 'performing' and reinvest it in another insurance policy.

The problem that investors face when they work with an adviser who is not an insurance agent is something similar: only the percentage of commissions earned is different. While an insurance company pays up 40% commission on the first premium of the policy, a PMS product sold by the bank fetches the relationship manager 3-4% commission on the day he sells you a PMS product and anywhere between 0.75-1% in the subsequent years. Hence the constant 'review' of your PMS and the advice to exit the product and reinvest it in a strategy that will give better returns.

The other structural issue with investment advisory business is that the adviser makes his commission irrespective of the performance of the investor's portfolio. Once an investor has invested, irrespective of the performance of the underlying investment, the adviser will continue to make money as long as the investor stays invested.

There is a difference between how this dynamic works for an insurance agent and how it works for advisers that allocate in non-insurance products. An insurance agent's commission has no bearing with the market value of your investment. Irrespective of the growth in the value of your investment or a fall in the value of your investment, the agent will make commission on the premium you pay.

In the case of financial products other than insurance, products like mutual funds and PMS, advisors get commissions on the market value of the investment. What is the market value of the investment?

Market value is the value at which you can sell your investment.

A portfolio of equity mutual funds and an equity PMS consists of investments made in shares listed on stock exchanges. As the price of these stocks changes so does the value of the portfolio. A fall in the prices of these stocks will reduce the market value of the investment and a rise in the value of these stocks will see the value of the portfolio appreciate. The advisers make commissions on the market value of this investment.

Yes, you are thinking on the right lines. The adviser stands to make more money if he is able to grow your portfolio. So, there is a part of the investment advisory process where there is an alignment of incentives. Investors and advisers both benefit from growth in the value of the amount invested.

We have so far discussed the need for a financial adviser and also discussed why the existing investment advisory business in India hasn't helped you achieve your financial goals. Let us now discuss how we can make the investment advisory business work to our benefit?

We start by asking if investors need an investment adviser. After all, we live in the age of information overload. What can an investment adviser tell you that you cannot find out on your own with a simple google search. Better still, you can open the YouTube app and India's finest financial experts will tell you how you can invest wisely and achieve FIRE.

FIRE, if you are hearing the term for the first time, means Financially Independent Retire Early. There are answers to all your questions packaged in five-minute videos and advice that can be implemented on an easy-to-use do-it-yourself app. Why then bother looking for an adviser from an industry that is anyway not designed to help you meet your financial goals.

The case for a financial advice can be built around the following points:

- They are a keeper of record, like a tool that captures your ever-changing financial goals and your proximity to those goals.

- They provide access to relevant and accurate information.

- They are an analyst who help you process all the relevant information and distil that information into actionable goals and measurable outcomes.

- They are the coach who can help you stay on track and dissuade you from taking irrational decisions in times of uncertainty and periods of euphoria or chaos in financial markets.

Let us start with the adviser's role as a keeper of your records. Intuitively it sounds like a very simple task. In its most simple form, this task is maintaining a simple excel sheet or a register of all your assets and liabilities and updating the value of those assets and liabilities at regular intervals. Yes, it is as simple as that.

Now ask yourself: have you been able to do this? Is there an app that you can open and see all your investments? Learn about the latest value of the LIC policy that you bought 16 years ago? The current value of the PPF account that your father opened for you when you started working? What is the balance of the employee provident fund account, the balance you are yet to transfer to your existing employer? What is the asset allocation of your portfolio? What is the maturity date of your fixed deposits? Who is the nominee in your LIC policy? Do you still want that person to be the nominee in your investments? What is the bank mandate in your first ELSS investment? Do you still use that bank account?

As the portfolio size grows and as the investor's life cycle stage changes, it becomes difficult to keep a track of investments and record them. Yes, there are apps available and you can do this yourself. Ask yourself why haven't you done this already? What stops you from doing it? The answer is – life.

Keeping a record of your assets and your liabilities is one of the many things that fill up your day. Most of your day is taken up by your job or the business you are running; you end up spending anything from 10 to 12 hours on work and commuting to and from your place of work. The weekend is spent taking care of the house, spending time with friends and family, and rest and recuperation. Before you know it, days, weeks and months go by and the only time you think of your investments is when something drastic happens in the stock market, or your friends talk about their portfolios, or you need to draw money from it. Otherwise *marne ki fursat nahin hai, portfolio kaun dekhega...* (there's no time to die, who'll check the portfolio!). This is our lived reality.

Life in India is an exercise in juggling too many balls, and recording or keeping of financial assets does not get the importance it deserves. Just as the urban Indians are careless with their health, and only start taking it seriously when hit by some health issue, they are not serious about their financial health as well, until struck by an unforeseen untoward event.

A well-designed portfolio statement that captures all your assets and liabilities, updated at regular intervals, is a must if you want to achieve your financial goals. What is not recorded, cannot be measured; what cannot be measured, cannot be tracked; and what is not tracked cannot be aligned or improved upon.

A good financial adviser will help you keep a record of your assets, liabilities and investments. The other critical function of a financial adviser is providing relevant and accurate information. There are over 40 assets management companies in India. Between them they offer over 1500 mutual fund schemes. There are over 100 scheduled commercial banks in India that offer fixed deposits of multiple tenures and at varying interest rates. The universe of listed stocks in India is over 2800 and the value of outstanding bonds in India is over 2 trillion dollars. There are over 200 PMS fund managers who run multiple fund management strategies. Indian fund managers now offer alternative investment funds that help clients do leveraged trades.

As our economy grows, financial markets and financial products will see innovation and the number of products and investment strategies available to investors will grow by leaps and bounds. Not only do the investors have access to umpteen investment options, they are also living in one of the most over-communicated societies in the world. The number of business news channels and newspapers in India is more than the number of such channels and newspapers in all of the English-speaking countries put together.

Then there is social media. A never-ending stream of experts telling investors everything they need to know about investing via their YouTube channels, free to join WhatsApp groups and exclusive Telegram channels. It can all be overwhelming. The skill to separate insight from the noise can be acquired but it takes time and in case of financial investments literally comes at a price. If one can cut through the clutter and identify the right source of information, it is difficult to discern the conflict of interest.

A good financial adviser helps you access the information you need in a time-bound and comprehensible manner. Financial markets have already taken it into account any information that is in the public domain. Once the event has played out – a war, a bank run or a pandemic – there is no point looking at the portfolio and wondering what could have been done. A financial adviser helps you design a portfolio after analysing all that has happened in the past, one that will stand the test of risks that future might bring. Yes, there are limits to how far anyone can see into the future; your adviser is also limited by her bounded rationality.

A good financial adviser helps by sharing with you lessons from history – the history of economic and financial cycles. They glean meaningful information that helps you understand the risks your portfolio carries. All relevant information is made available to you in a timely and precise manner. What next? A good financial adviser will use this information to design a portfolio that will help you meet your financial goals. Your goals and objectives can be categorised as short-term, medium-term and long-term goals. A short-term goal could be buying a car, a medium-term goal could be buying a house and a long-term goal could be building a retirement corpus. Each of these goals needs a specific asset allocation that needs to be constantly monitored and revised.

Not only are the asset classes different for different financial goals, they are also impacted by economic variables and developments in the capital markets on an ongoing basis. One may argue that investors can themselves track these developments and ensure that the asset allocation is in line with the stated financial goals. Of course they can, but how many can take out the time for this, given the lives they live, as discussed earlier.

There is no dearth of free tools that can help investors track the movement of asset classes in their portfolio on a daily basis. Our modern world is nothing if not a world of 'free' internet-powered tools that help us solve all problems. But do the investors have the time, the skill sets and the motivation to use all these tools and meet their financial goals. 'Do It Yourself' or get a professional to do it is the question. If you think, as an investor you have the skill set, the time and the motivation to process all the information and take appropriate action at the right time, then the Do It Yourself process is for you. My lived experience in India has made it impossible to live a Do-It-Yourself life.

If there is one thing that we get in India in abundance, it is access to cheap labour. Take a pause and think of your friends and family members who live outside India. Especially those who live in the US, Canada, Western Europe or Australia. They not only do the cooking and cleaning of their homes themselves, they also wash their cars, do basic household plumbing, assemble furniture that they buy from IKEA and some even do basic car repairs and painting of their house.

How many of these tasks do we do here in India? There is a good chance that you have never changed the washer of a tap, repaired your cell phone or bought furniture that you have assembled at home. In India we always find someone to do these tasks for us at a price we can afford. We have access to people who can do all these tasks for us at prices we can afford. This helps us put in long hours at the office, on commutes and spend weekends with our families. Add to this the relative complexity of the financial markets and the economic environment they operate in and we as investors need help for investments to grow and help us achieve our financial goals.

A good financial adviser is a coach – someone who has been there and done that. She is somebody who has invested her money and advised clients over multiple economic and financial market cycles. A deep correction in the stock market, when the market falls greater than 20% in a short period of time, is caused by a major economic, financial or political event. It is easy to say, and write in a book, to maintain the discipline of asset allocation. It is easy for me to write: If your equity portfolio has seen a drawdown of 20% you should invest in the stock market and rebalance your portfolio.

It is easy to say and write in a book that the value of your equity portfolio has grown 100% in the last one year and that it is time to re-balance it.

Please be mindful that booking gains in your equity portfolio and reinvesting the profits in another equity mutual fund scheme, which will give better returns than your current equity mutual fund scheme, is not rebalancing of the portfolio. Portfolio rebalancing means booking profits in an asset class and reinvesting those gains in another asset class.

Fear and greed are two emotions that drive our investments behaviour. When the stock market falls by 20%, the reasons for its fall sound obvious. Nobody saw the risks that led to the fall of stock markets by 20% a month before the stock market fell. Now everyone is an expert on why the stock market will continue to go down. There is consensus all around that this time it is different. That stock market will not go up again. This is a crisis that the world has never seen before.

Recall the stock markets crash of March 2020. The world was shutting down. Nobody had any clue as to when we will go back to offices, what will happen to businesses and the economy, how the crisis will end. As I write this in 2025, all that seems like a distant memory.

The stock markets not only recovered from their lows of March 2020, they also saw an unprecedented bull run that started in April 2020 and culminated in November 2021. By the middle of 2021, not only had the stock markets shrugged off Covid-induced lockdowns, public and private equity markets were flooded with liquidity and investors were buying stocks at valuations that could only be justified with unrealistic assumptions of earning growth.

Just like fear had gripped the investors in March 2020, by July 2021 investors had thrown all caution to wind, showing a callous disregard for valuations and buying risky assets that all but assured that their portfolios would underperform. A good financial adviser helps you retain balance.

She does not let all pervasive negativity that prevents you from investing when the discipline of asset allocation demands you invest bother you and neither does she let the euphoria sway you when the noise in and around the capital markets will tell you that stocks will continue to go up and that you need not bother rebalancing your portfolio.

A good financial adviser is that experienced voice and that firm hand that keeps you disciplined and helps you navigate in times of turbulence in the markets and pulls you out of the party when everyone has convinced you that this time it is different and the music will not stop. We have now built the case for a financial adviser.

The question that follows from this is how do we identify the right investment adviser and how does one gauge the efficacy and the financial advice and how does one keep the financial adviser accountable? In the earlier part of this chapter, we discussed how financial advisers have let down investors and how your personal experience has been no different when it comes to poor financial advice. We discussed the incentive structures that drive the financial advisory business and how there is a conflict of interest. Advisers want you to invest in products that give them high upfront commissions. While choosing the investment product for the client, their focus is not on the suitability of the product but on how much commissions they will make out of the sale. The key lies in finding an adviser whose financial incentives are in line with your financial goals.

How can an investor align the financial incentives of her portfolio and those of her investment adviser? What are the characteristics of a good financial adviser? Should investors have institutions as their adviser, a bank or a wealth management company that designates a staff member to advise. The representative advises on the basis of the advisory framework laid out by the organisation and does what the company tells him to do.

Should the investor opt for a standalone financial adviser? What are the advantages and disadvantages of these models? What are the regulatory requirements that help investors in safeguarding their interests? The characteristics of a good financial adviser encompass what we discussed in the section on the role of a good financial adviser. Let us build on that.

Financial advisory business in India is regulated by Securities and Exchange Board of India (SEBI). SEBI plays the same role in the wealth management industry that the Reserve Bank of India plays in the banking sector. It regulates the functioning of investment managers like mutual funds and portfolio management service providers and also regulates the activities of financial advisers and distributors of financial products. Here it must be noted that SEBI does not regulate insurance companies. Insurance companies and distribution of insurance products in India are regulated by Insurance Development and Regulatory Authority of India Ltd (IDRA).

SEBI and IRDA stipulate that any professional working as a financial adviser, in her own capacity or as a representative of an organisation, needs to register with them. As part of the registration process the adviser has to clear the certification examination as per the rules and the syllabus laid out by the concerned regulator. In India, an individual cannot work as a financial adviser or distributor of financial products till he or she has cleared the relevant examination and has registered themselves with the regulator. The examination tests the prospective adviser on the knowledge and understanding of various financial products.

A checklist for identifying the right financial adviser should start with checking on the various financial regulators the adviser is registered with and for how long they have been registered to work as a financial adviser. Once the investor has established that the adviser is registered with a regulator the next step should be to check the access the adviser has to data and information relevant to economy and capital markets. Banks and companies operating in the wealth management business have dedicated product teams that work on compiling all this information and disseminating it to their colleagues working as advisors. Financial advisers representing these organisations have access to information and data they need to give the right advice.

The data and information are available to all, through a combination of open source and free data sources and paid subscriptions. An adviser working independently can also access this information. In the case of an independent financial adviser, the onus is on the adviser to not just access the data but also to process it and produce meaningful information. This means an independent financial adviser does the role of an investment specialist as well. This is a critical difference between advisers working for institutions and those working independently. The former can rely on experience and expertise that the institution has built over the years but their own understanding of the investment products is limited.

The financial advisers representing institutions are akin to salesmen that you encounter in shops and other business establishments. Advisers representing banks and financial institutions are trained to follow the advisory process that their organisation follows and are not expected to apply their understanding of financial markets and products and advise clients accordingly. Since they are agents of the organisation they do as they are told and their incentives are linked to the incentives of their organisation. This is the reason why your bank relationship manager is always asking you to invest in an insurance product. She has been trained to sell you that insurance product by her bank and has not been given the leeway to design a portfolio that will help you achieve your financial goals. All her understanding of financial markets and financial products is useless because she is representing an organisation that has decided that a life insurance product is what you need and any customisation of your portfolio is frowned upon.

An independent financial adviser is an entrepreneur; she spends time enhancing her understanding of financial products and border economic trends and gets to design her own framework of financial advisory. An independent financial advisor gets to set her own incentive structure with the clients and has all the flexibility to work in the way she thinks is the right way to work with her clients, unencumbered by profits of a large organisation.

This brings us to the elephant in the room. How can the investor align the interest of her portfolio with the commercial interests of the financial advisor? In my experience as a wealth manager for over 15 years, this alignment is difficult to set in place because the clients are averse to the idea of treating the financial adviser the way they treat their doctor, chartered accountant, or a lawyer, a professional who provides a valued skill set and deserves to be suitably compensated for the service the adviser provides. A financial adviser does not hold a degree that is considered difficult to acquire, like a degree in medicine or law and does not need the rigour of certification that a chartered accountant needs. The ease of entry in the financial advisory profession gives clients the impression that financial advisory is not a specialised skill.

As we have discussed in the earlier sections of this book, on the face of it, a good financial advisory is a combination of getting the basics right and maintaining discipline. A good financial plan and its execution do not entail everyday execution of instructions. Once the plan has been put in place and action on it taken, the work of the adviser is to monitor and this often means not doing anything. That your financial adviser is not making you invest or redeem or reinvest every three months does not mean she is not doing her work. The work of your financial adviser after a point is akin to the work of your office's security set-up. Just because the guards at the reception are not apprehending intruders every hour does not mean they are not doing their work and are not needed. They were put in place after doing a thorough review of the security requirements and have been stationed at their respective positions as part of that plan. That they end up standing there all day doing nothing does not mean they are not working.

As individuals we get this and are comfortable with the idea of bearing the cost of this security set-up, but as investors we are not comfortable with idea of paying a fee to an adviser or the adviser earning a commission on the portfolio if the adviser does nothing other than send you a portfolio statement once a month and does not give you a trading tip or an investment idea at regular intervals. It makes us question the value of the service that is being provided.

We go to a dinner with friends or a social do and hear our friends tell stories of how their adviser helped them make money on a particular stock or how she made them invest in an idea that has doubled their money and we start to ask ourselves if the financial adviser is doing her job. Why is it that you are not told of new product ideas? We begin to question the aptitude and intelligence of the financial adviser and soon start looking for someone who is always ready with a new investment idea. The other side of this dynamic is the inability of financial advisers to inspire confidence in the service that they deliver.

Financial advisers do not get treated the way investors treat their doctors or lawyers because most financial advisers do not demonstrate the skill sets and the aptitude necessary to deliver the financial advice that works for their clients. They avoid the conversation that lays out explicitly the fee they will charge their clients or the commissions that they will make because that would entail explicitly laying down their role and responsibilities and implementing a framework where the financial adviser can be held accountable for not delivering on her side of the arrangement.

The financial adviser is unable to generate confidence in the client of his or her ability to deliver on the client's financial goals and ends up discussing specific product ideas instead of drawing a holistic plan that takes into account the goals and objectives of the client and ends up behaving like a product salesman. Since the investors end up getting the impression that they are being sold an investment product, they treat the adviser as one and we end up in this vicious cycle of distrust. Add to this scenario the fact that the advisers do not participate in any drawdowns or the losses that the portfolio may see and ask for a fee and earn commissions irrespective of how the portfolio performs and the alignment of incentives never happens. The solution is simple but has not taken off in India at scale.

The solution is a transparent arrangement between the adviser and the investor on the fee and commissions that the adviser will get for the services delivered. The figure could be a fixed fee or a percentage of the value of the investments that the adviser gets to advise on. This needs a change of mindset on behalf of the investors. The issue is because the investor is paying for an intangible product; one can't touch and feel financial advice. The financial adviser does not turn up on your door every day and demonstrate what she does to deserve her compensation, like your yoga instructor or fitness trainer does. The impact of her advice is not instant unlike the medication that the doctor has prescribed for you. To write out a cheque for a once-in-a-quarter meeting at the end of which no action is taken calls for a different mindset.

Mutual funds in India offer two kinds of plans – direct and regular plans. Everything about these plans is similar; the only difference is the expense. Direct plans have lower fund management changes vis-à-vis regular plans. An adviser makes her commission from the excess expense that the fund manager charges on under the regular plan. An investor can invest in direct plans of the mutual fund schemes easily and save on the extra expense. To let the adviser earn her commission by continuing to invest in regular plans needs a mindset that values sound advice. The arrangement can only work if advisers in turn deliver on their side of the bargain.

The process of advisory should be clearly communicated to the clients; advisers need to expend time and energy on explaining to the client the various financial models that they have considered before designing the portfolio. Clients should be communicated the qualification and the experience that advisers bring to the table, and also the access to resources that the adviser has at the time of designing the portfolio. The adviser should also share the methodology for portfolio reviews, the frequency of reviews and the triggers for changing the portfolio if and when a change is needed. If the advisers want to get treated like other professionals they need to deliver like other professionals. From my personal experience as a wealth manager, I can assure you that clients do not grudge the fee or income advisers make as long as they see the advisers delivering sound advice and helping clients achieve their financial goals.

The alignment of interests can be achieved, provided the adviser is transparent and clients are confident they will not be taken for a ride. Clients, over a period of time, through a painfully iterative process, will find the right adviser. The onus is on the advisers that the iterative process ends at them and clients do not go on looking for the right adviser.

If you are an investor, think of finding the right adviser as finding the right therapist for yourself or the right career counsellor for your children. The right professional is worth every paisa you will pay her. If you are an adviser treat your client's assets like you would treat your own or your *parents ka corpus* (or as that of the corpus of your parents). Do that and you will find that not only do the clients trust you and are willing to pay you a fee, they will also refer you to their friends and family. If you are an investor, I hope this chapter has helped you define your financial adviser and your terms of engagement with her. If you are a Financial Adviser, I hope this chapter has given you food for thought.

Summary: A good financial adviser will help you take risks, build a diversified portfolio for you, help you maintain discipline of asset allocation and deliver the benefits of compounding. You need to work with your adviser and ensure there is no conflict of interest. As an investor you should be comfortable with the idea of a professional adviser earning a fee just like you are comfortable with your family doctor, accountant or lawyer making his fee. Align the fee income that your adviser makes with the services she delivers and it's a win-win for you and your adviser.

7

Living within One's Means

Our lives are all about consumption. It is the purpose of the modern world and capitalist societies to make us consume. We are told our expense is someone else's income. Everything around us nudges us to answer two questions.

1.   How do we look?
2.   How much money do we make?

There is a constant pressure on us to seek external validation. It's not just with friends and family, we are pressured to live up to the expectations of the world at large. People often worry about how do they look, what brands they wear, as if the whole purpose of life is to consume. The next vacation, the latest iPhone, another dress are also things that are frequently on people's minds to project an enhanced status. Every day we are subjected to mass marketing campaigns that tell us to consume. Endless consumption needs an endless source of income.

If you think you are not earning enough, there is always a loan on offer – a personal loan that will help you take that next vacation, a loan to help you buy the latest smartphone. A whole industry has sprung up BNPL – Buy Now Pay Later. Yes, credit is the foundation of modern economies and your investments will not deliver the returns you expect if people don't borrow and spend. Your bank is able to offer you a rate of interest because someone is borrowing from your bank at a rate of interest higher than your fixed deposit rate. Your investments have businesses that make profits by lending money for consumption.

There is the paradigm of YOLO – You Only Live Once – so live it up. Live in the moment; life is so uncertain why defer consumption when one does not even know if there is a tomorrow. I am a part of this environment and enjoy 'finer' things in life myself. What I always try to do is manage the low probability high impact risks that we are susceptible to. Modern tools of risk management that depend on financial assets are great but one must not forget the lessons that conventional wisdom and tradition have taught us.

Not all risk management needs an excel sheet; sometimes the accumulated experience of centuries of survival is enough. The Indian subcontinent is home to 4000 years of uninterrupted civilisation. What lessons can we learn from this success? India is a success. It has lasted the test of time. Anything that lasts this long has accumulated experience and has managed risk efficiently.

In North India we often hear a Hindi saying: *Tete paon pasaria, jeti lambi saur.* Here is a literal translation: As you sleep stretch your legs only as far as your blanket. It means one should live within one's means, and not stretch their finances. The point is not to avoid debt.

Access to low-interest home loans has been one of the biggest drivers of growth in India in the past three decades. The average age of first-time home buyers in India is now in 30s; earlier the average age of home buyers in India used to be in 40s. The boom in housing demand, fuelled by access to credit has had a multiplier impact on our economy lifting everyone up. The point I make here is that the borrowing for consumption that does not lead to asset creation should be avoided. Personal loan for a vacation, swiping that credit card for an impulse purchase at a mall and buying the latest smartphone for which you will pay an EMI for next 24 months is stretching your finances. An EMI will remain irrespective of your ability to pay it. Borrowing to consume today instead of saving today and consuming tomorrow is not a savvy way of managing one's money.

Look around and think of the people whose financial acumen you admire. Ask them how much debt they have on their personal balance sheet. Do they revolve on their credit card? When was the last time they borrowed to spend money on an experience or

borrowed to spend on something that was not a necessity for them? Just because it is available and accessible does not mean you need it.

Any debt that does not help you strengthen your balance sheet should be avoided. Anybody who shows you magic of modern finance and makes you believe otherwise either does not understand risk or is trying to sell you…a loan.

Living within your means is the first and most important step in achieving financial goals. The key to 'financial freedom' is not the strength of your balance sheet; it is the length of your expense sheet. Don't take my word for it, see what your family has believed

for centuries. They are right because their decisions have got you to a place where you have the privilege of reading this sentence.

Wishing you years of good financial health ahead.

Summary: The key to 'financial freedom' is not the strength of your balance sheet; it is the length of your expense sheet. It is the length of your expense sheet and the rate at which it is growing that will define your financial freedom.

Glossary

Bonds: Bonds are a type of fixed income instrument where the investor lends the issuer money in return of interest. The issuer can be governments or corporations. Money is lent for a predetermined time period. Bonds once issued can be listed on the exchange and bought and sold via the exchange.

BSE 500: The BSE 500 is an index that represents 500 companies listed on the Bombay Stock Exchange (BSE). It is a broad stock market index that includes companies from large, mid, and small cap segments across various sectors, providing a comprehensive view of the Indian equity market. It is used as a benchmark to measure the overall stock market performance, as it includes a wide and diverse basket of stocks.

Debt Mutual Funds: Mutual Fund schemes that invest in fixed income instruments are called Debt Mutual Funds.

Equity Investment: An investment in a business. Investors are called shareholders and receive a share certificate or shares in their demat account in exchange of the money they invest in the business.

Equity Mutual Funds: Mutual fund schemes that invest in equity instruments are called Equity Mutual Funds.

Fixed Income Instruments: A financial asset that defines the rate of return and tenure of the investment the moment investment is made. A bank fixed deposit is a fixed income instrument. Fixed deposits and bonds are examples of fixed income instruments.

Gold Mutual Fund: Mutual Fund schemes that invest in gold are called Gold Mutual Funds.

Index Fund: Index mutual funds are mutual fund schemes that aim to replicate the performance of a specific stock market index, such as the Nifty 50 or a BSE 500.

Inflation: Increase in the prices of goods and services. Inflation reduces the purchasing power of money.

Multi Asset Allocation Fund: Mutual fund schemes that invest in a combination of equity, fixed income and commodities multi asset allocation funds. Government rules specify that for a scheme to qualify as a multi asset allocation scheme, it needs to invest a minimum of 10% of its assets under management in each of these categories.

Mutual Fund: An investment vehicle through which investors can invest in equity and fixed income instruments. They receive units in exchange for the amount invested. Their money is managed by a professional fund manager. Mutual Funds DO NOT GUARANTEE RETURNS. Legally no mutual fund scheme can offer guaranteed returns.

Nominal Return: Nominal return is the return that an investment generates. A 395 days bank deposit that gives 7% return is delivering a 7% nominal return.

NSE Nifty 50 Index: NSE Nifty 50 is the benchmark index of the Indian stock market. The NSE Nifty 50 consists of stocks of the 50 largest and most liquid companies listed on India's National Stock Exchange (NSE).

Portfolio Management Service: Portfolio Management Services (PMS) refers to an investment service where professional portfolio managers manage investors through direct ownership of stocks or any other asset in the investor's name. This is unlike mutual funds where investments are pooled into a shared fund. The structure of the PMS enables a customised investment approach that can be tailored to every unique investor's risk tolerance, preferences and objectives.

Real Return: Nominal return minus the rate of inflation is a real return. If the rate of inflation is 5%, the aforesaid fixed deposit is delivering a real return of 2%.

Risk: The possibility of the investment not delivering the expected return is called risk. The uncertain nature of the outcome makes all decision-making risky. Risk in investments could entail failure of the investment to generate the return that the investors expect and or loss of the principal invested.

Volatility: Change in the value of an asset over a given period of time. Higher the volatility of an asset's price, the more difficult it is to time cash flows from that investment.

About the Author

Maneesh Taneja is an Investment Adviser based in Gurgaon. In a wealth management career spanning over seventeen years he has worked in wealth management divisions of Citibank, 360 One Wealth and Axis Bank. He helps high net worth individuals and institutions manage their money and achieve their financial goals. Maneesh did his Post Graduate Diploma in Management from T. A. Pai Management Institute, Manipal and holds NISM VA-Mutual Funds Distributor Certificate, NISM XXIA-Portfolio Management Services Distributor Certificate and NISM XIII Common Derivatives Certification.

You can follow Maneesh on Instagram @7steps2financialfreedom.